Games for the Whole Child

Brian Barrett, PhD

**HUMAN
KINETICS**

Library of Congress Cataloging-in-Publication Data

Barrett, Brian, 1956-
Games for the whole child / Brian Barrett.
  p. cm.
Includes bibliographical references.
ISBN 0-7360-5343-3 (soft cover)
1. Educational games. 2. Movement education. 3. Holistic education. I. Title.
GV1480.B26 2005
371.33'7—dc22   2004021839

ISBN: 0-7360-5343-3

The Web addresses cited in this text were current as of September 13, 2004, unless otherwise noted.

Acquisitions Editor: Gayle Kassing; **Developmental Editor:** Jennifer M. Sekosky; **Assistant Editor:** Ragen E. Sanner; **Copyeditor:** Alisha Jeddeloh; **Proofreader:** Julie Marx Goodreau; **Permission Manager:** Dalene Reeder; **Graphic Designer:** Nancy Rasmus; **Graphic Artist:** Angela K. Snyder; **Cover Designer:** Keith Blomberg; **Photographer (cover):** Kelly J. Huff; **Art Manager:** Kelly Hendren; **Illustrator:** Keri J. Evans; **Printer:** Versa Press

Printed in the United States of America
10   9   8   7   6   5   4   3   2   1

Human Kinetics
Web site: www.HumanKinetics.com

United States: Human Kinetics
P.O. Box 5076
Champaign, IL 61825-5076
800-747-4457
e-mail: humank@hkusa.com

Canada: Human Kinetics
475 Devonshire Road Unit 100
Windsor, ON N8Y 2L5
800-465-7301 (in Canada only)
e-mail: orders@hkcanada.com

Europe: Human Kinetics
107 Bradford Road
Stanningley
Leeds LS28 6AT, United Kingdom
+44 (0) 113 255 5665
e-mail: hk@hkeurope.com

Australia: Human Kinetics
57A Price Avenue
Lower Mitcham, South Australia 5062
08 8277 1555
e-mail: liaw@hkaustralia.com

New Zealand: Human Kinetics
Division of Sports Distributors NZ Ltd.
P.O. Box 300 226 Albany
North Shore City
Auckland
0064 9 448 1207
e-mail: blairc@hknewz.com

I would like to dedicate this book to my mother Lois, my daughter Rose, and my friend, mentor and teacher, Marianne Torbert. To mom for teaching me to persevere and teaching me that I could do whatever I set out to do. To Rose who teaches me everyday how much fun it is to run, play, and have an imagination. To Dr. Marianne Torbert (Temple University) who changed my life as a physical educator and has changed the lives of countless students.

Finally a word of thanks to Dr. Gayle Kassing, Jennifer Sekosky, and Ragen Sanner of Human Kinetics for organizing and giving better direction to what was at first a manuscript that needed help.

Contents

Activity Finder

Name of game	Page	NASPE standards	Type of game
Ahhh Bucket!	108	2, 3, 4, 5, 6	Group initiative
All Mixed Up	134	1, 2, 5, 6	Group initiative
All Tied Up	48	2, 3, 4, 5, 6	Fitness
Around the World Basketball	90	1, 2, 3, 4, 5, 6	Sport
Baseball or Kickball	92	1, 2, 5 ,6	Sport
Big Wheel	110	2, 3, 4, 5, 6	Group initiative
Bleachers and Bench	50	1, 2, 3, 4, 5, 6	Fitness
Botkey	30	1, 2, 3, 4, 5, 6	Skill practice
Bottle Blast	28	1, 2, 5	Skill practice
Bottle-Cap Football	94	1, 2, 3, 4, 5, 6	Sport
Bottle Rockets	52	1, 2, 3, 4, 5, 6	Fitness
Boxball	32	1, 2, 3, 4, 5, 6	Skill practice
Bring Back My Body	20	2, 3, 4, 5, 6	Warm-up
Capture the Flag	53	1, 2, 3, 4, 5, 6	Fitness
Carry On	114	2, 3, 4, 5, 6	Group initiative
Chicken and the Coyote, The	56	2, 3, 4, 5, 6	Fitness
Cliffhanger	112	2, 3, 4, 5, 6	Group initiative
Cone Tipping	58	1, 2, 3, 4, 5, 6	Fitness
Crossover Volleyball	102	1, 2, 5, 6	Sport
Dee Fence	62	1, 2, 3, 4, 5, 6	Fitness
Egg Beater	24	1, 2, 3, 4, 5, 6	Warm-up
Foot Fencing	63	1, 2, 3, 4, 5, 6	Fitness
Four-Way Tug	87	1, 2, 3, 4, 5, 6	Fitness
French Fries and Frankfurters	60	1, 2, 3, 4, 5, 6	Fitness
Geography Dodgeball	34	1, 2, 5, 6	Skill practice
Give 'n' Go	44	1, 2, 3, 4, 5, 6	Skill practice
Globetrotters	36	1, 2, 5, 6	Skill practice
Good, the Bad and the Healthy, The	65	1, 2, 3, 4, 5, 6	Fitness
Grass Hockey	96	1, 2, 3, 4, 5, 6	Sports
Half-Pipe	120	2, 3, 4, 5, 6	Group initiative

(continued)

(continued)

Preface

Enough already! Stop with the boring push-ups, sit-ups, and laps. Such activities do a poor job of meeting the physical needs of children and don't address their social, emotional, or cognitive needs at all. Instead of treating children as a collection of isolated parts, we need to treat them as whole individuals, teaching them activities that meet all their needs.

This book is ultimately about the promotion of physical activity. However, its approach is unique. Instead of teaching children to exercise three to five days per week for 20 to 60 minutes at a certain percentage of their maximum heart rate, this book offers games that develop children socially, emotionally, and cognitively as well as physically.

When activities address the whole child, they become intrinsically motivating. Children want to repeat the movement experience time and time again, now and for a lifetime. Combining developmental needs into a holistic educational approach is called whole-child learning.

Why do we need this holistic approach? Considering the overwhelming number of active children in the United States and the equally overwhelming number of sedentary adults, it is obvious that somewhere along the way physical education, recreation, and sport programs have missed the boat.

Decades of calisthenics did not produce active adults because such activities did not meet the needs of children. Likewise, it is doubtful that the present trend of having children run laps, take heart rates, and use pedometers will produce lifetime movers. Jogging laps meets a physical need, but it does not address social, emotional, or cognitive needs. Tracking daily pedometer counts meets a cognitive need, but nothing else. We need to capitalize on children's innate drive to move so that we can create lifetime movers who receive all the health benefits of an active lifestyle.

What you will find in this book are 61 highly enjoyable games that allow children to make decisions, communicate, share ideas and equipment, help others, listen to others, and participate at their own level. These are just some of the unique needs of children that this book addresses.

We need to keep children turned on to movement for as long as possible—ideally, for a lifetime. Activities that allow children to negotiate develop *social* skills. Games that allow children to select their level of participation provide a sense of belonging, filling an *emotional* need. Children who are allowed to plan, develop strategies, and generate alternatives are working on *cognitive* skills. Games in which children move a large muscle mass sporadically, bend, twist, push, and pull to meet their *physical* needs.

When children are exposed to physical activity that they find interesting and that meets all their needs, they discover that movement makes them feel good. This emotional connection with movement causes children to repeat the experience and in the process reap health benefits. *Games for the Whole Child* explores this concept of using games to address childhood development needs. The games in this book are designed for children in kindergarten through eighth grade, but several can also be used with high school students and adults.

I have used the games in this book for more than 10 years. Research has been conducted on the level of enjoyment (see table C.1 on p. 150 for results) and heart-rate response to several of the activities in this book (see table 1.1 on p. 8 for results). The games and activities are divided into five chapters: (1) Warm-Up Games, (2) Skill Practice, (3) Fitness Games, (4) Sport Games, and (5) Group Initiatives. Here are some ways to use the games:

- Physical educators who want a workout can select a game from the warm-ups, move to a cardiorespiratory or strength game from the fitness section, and close the class with a skill-practice activity.
- Coaches can spice up drill and skill practices using nontraditional sports as well as skill-practice activities.
- Recreation leaders and camp counselors can help children bond using ideas from the group initiatives section (chapter 6). Summer recreation leaders will find quick activities that are easy to implement in the extra minutes during the transition from one main activity to another.
- Supervisors of before- and after-school programs will find activities that require little or no equipment.

These are just a few of the many ways the games from this book can be implemented. Each individual situation may require modifications, some of which have been anticipated. Group leaders know their players best and should use activities suited to their players.

Those of us lucky enough to work with children must put their needs above all else. Activities that reduce the fear of failure, eliminate elimination, allow for participation at different ability levels, and avoid boring adult exercise are important—they are *fun*. But never forget that the adult leader who is genuinely playful is also important to any game's success.

Acknowledgments

I would like to take this opportunity to thank several people.

Many of the games in this book are variations of games found in other books. Modifications have been made to make the games more inclusive and more enjoyable, and they have been analyzed to meet specific objectives. There are also those games that came from teachers, mentors, and friends. Unfortunately, many ideas have come from shared conversations over lunch or after a workshop session, and I have forgotten the names of some of these folks.

Thanks go to the following people:

Marianne Torbert, PhD (director of the Leonard Gordon Institute for Human Development Through Play, of Temple University, author of *Follow Me*, published by P.L.A.Y. Resource Center)

Gene White, PhD (East Stroudsburg University)

Curt Hinson, PhD (author of *Fitness for Children*, published by Human Kinetics)

Ambrose Brazelton (author of *I may be little, but I'm big inside*, Great Activities Publishing, and *Clap, snap and tap,* Educational Record Center)

Stephen Virgilio, PhD (author of *Fitness Education for Children*, Human Kinetics)

Emily R. Foster, Karyn Hartinger, and Katherine A. Smith (authors of *Fitness Fun*, Human Kinetics)

Robert Pangrazi, PhD (author of *Dynamic physical education for elementary school children*, 11th edition, Allyn and Bacon)

Jim McCann (Gloucester Township Schools, New Jersey)

Karl Rohnke (author of *Silver Bullets* and *Cowtails and Cobras II*, Project Adventure Inc.)

Victor Addonizio (physical educator, Lafayette Mills Elementary, Manalapan, NJ)

How To Use This Book

Each of the 61 games in this book falls into one of five categories: warm-ups, skill practice, fitness, sport games, and group initiatives. Regardless of the category, all activities meet the social, emotional, cognitive, and physical needs of children. Each game has icons representing these four needs.

- **Social**

- **Emotional**

- **Cognitive**

- **Physical**

    Fitness   **Sport**

    Skill

Physical development is divided into two icons, fitness and skill objectives. Some games have five icons, meaning that those games have both physical objectives.

Numbers under each icon direct you to appendix A, where you'll find more detailed information on how each developmental need is met.

All of the games are designed to help you meet the national standards set by the National Association for Sport and Physical Education (NASPE). Within each game there is a listing of which standards apply. The standards can be found in appendix A.

Each game description also includes

- whether the game should be played indoors, outdoors, or either;
- necessary equipment;
- size of the play space;
- the setup of the play area; and
- a description of how to play.

The Strategies for Success component gives tips for making the game meet the divergent social, emotional, cognitive, and physical needs of the group. Several activities have a final section called Think About It. The comments and questions in this section are intended to focus your thoughts on the philosophy behind each game. As this understanding develops you will be better able to create and modify other games.

Please keep in mind that the suggested size of the play space is just that, a suggestion. The 40- by 60-foot (12- by 18-meter) measurement for the play space represents only half of my gymnasium. Game leaders work in all different conditions (larger or smaller gyms, cafeterias, classrooms, asphalt slabs) and should adapt the games to the play space available. No matter what amount of space is available, keep boundaries in running games away from walls, bleachers, fences, trees, and so on, and always check the space for hazards such as holes or broken glass.

There are several human-target activities in the book. I am well aware of the controversy surrounding such games. Thirty years ago dodgeball and bombardment-type games were often played with 8.5-inch (21.5-centimeter) rubber kickballs or worse. These balls caused many physical injuries and who knows how many emotional injuries. Each human-target activity in this book uses very soft, uncoated foam balls; yarn balls; or fleece balls. Any teacher philosophically opposed to such activities should simply move on to another game. My own experience using these modified human-target games has been a positive one.

Finally, if you are interested in finding out how much your students enjoyed a particular game, ask them. A worksheet for grading the game is available in appendix C.

Keep reading—the *fun* is just beginning!

Developing Games for the Whole Child

Children attend math class for cognitive development, go to an after-school club to develop social skills, get smiley faces on their homework to improve emotional well-being, and go to the gym to run laps for physical fitness. Traditional education reduces children to individual, separate needs. This book offers an alternative, one in which the whole child is taught the whole time.

Children are not adults in smaller bodies. This concept sounds simple, and not many educators would disagree. Yet our society seems determined to place younger and younger children into adult or age-inappropriate situations. Music, television, movies, and clothing are all examples of the ways in which adult content has filtered into childhood. Exercise, recreation, and children's sports are no exception.

Gone are the days when kids donned a T-shirt and ball cap for their Little League team, which practiced once a week. Today's Little Leaguers wear professional uniforms with team names and emblems and practice several times a week. Activities from ballet to soccer dominate the free time of children so that there is little time left for play. To promote an active lifestyle, professionals have imposed adult exercise principles on children's exercise programs.

Adult exercise programs are designed to fit the busy lives of adults, who find it more convenient to work out in one 30- to 60-minute session. School-age children, on the other hand, have more time and can easily spread their exercise throughout the day, yet children's programs often imitate adult programs at the local gym. Socially, children are just learning how to work effectively in groups. Emotionally, they need to develop a positive sense of self-worth. Cognitively, they are learning to think more abstractly.

Children enjoy playing games. When properly designed, games can provide all the physical benefits of adult programs and at the same time meet the unique social, emotional, and cognitive needs of children.

This chapter takes a look at using physical activities to help children develop socially, emotionally, cognitively, and physically. It points out the physical differences in children that make physical activities suited for children, rather than adults, necessary. It also addresses fundamentals of game planning. We begin by exploring the whole-child education movement.

The Whole-Child Philosophy

Whole-child education, or what some call holistic education, has been around for a long time, even dating as far back as Plato's time. Plato believed that education should address a young person's mind, body, and sense of aesthetics.

In the late 1800s, we met John Dewey, a giant in educational philosophy (*The School and Societe*, 1899; *Democracy and Education*, 1916). Dewey believed in learning by doing and adapting the curriculum to meet the needs of the learners, and he specifically did not support the dualism of separating mind and body. Dewey advocated the development of the whole person—mind, body, and soul.

The influence of John Dewey continued to be seen in the 1900s through a dominant force in physical education by the name of Jesse F. Williams, MD. Williams (*The Principles of Physical Education*, 1927; *Physical Education in the Elementary School*, 1951) was well known for advocating the idea that physical education was education both of and through the physical. He also believed in the physical, intellectual, and social development of the individual.

Each of these educators believed that education should cover more than traditional academic subjects, or as we say, the whole child. What makes up the whole child often varies according to the bias of the person proposing the definition. However, the list usually includes social, emotional, intellectual, physical, spiritual, creative, and artistic development. Although the physical is included here, many omit it from the list.

The National Association for the Education of Young Children (NAEYC) advocates that primary schools promote the social, emotional, cognitive, and physical development of all children: "Development in one dimension influences and is influenced by development in other dimensions. This premise is violated when schools place a great emphasis on the cognitive domain while minimizing other aspects of children's development. Because development cannot be neatly separated into parts, failure to attend to all aspects of an individual child's development is often the root cause of a child's failure in school" (NAEYC 1987).

Not everyone agrees. Physical educators Pate and Hohn (1994) believe it is foolhardy for physical education to take on the social or cognitive development of children. They believe that the main purpose of physical education is to promote an active lifestyle. This book proposes development of an active lifestyle, but it contends that this is not possible unless the movement experiences meet students' social, emotional, and cognitive needs in addition to meeting their physical needs. Elementary school children do not need to separate learning into the four domains; activities should address each area simultaneously.

We are not going to develop lifelong movers by teaching children the importance of fitness and how to plan a personal fitness program. That can wait until they're older. While children are running around playing Capture the Flag (page 54) their heart rate is elevated, but they're also planning strategies, evaluating strategies, helping others, developing a sense of belonging, and participating at their own level. They are learning that it feels good to move. They are having a great time, which is the result of having their needs met. Socially, the children are part of a team, working toward a common goal; emotionally they make contributions to their team at their own level; cognitively they choose their level and they make plans and evaluate them; and physically they run in a childlike run-rest-run-rest pattern. This is an example of whole-child learning.

Let us now turn to the specific social, emotional, cognitive, and physical needs of children.

Social and Emotional Needs

A fifth-grade physical education lesson on traditional volleyball had just ended. As the students filed out the door, a young girl muttered that she hated volleyball. At the following class, in an attempt to alter this child's negative perceptions, I allowed children who wanted to bump and set to do so. Others could catch, toss to themselves, and then bump or set, while others could catch the ball and toss it over the net as in Newcomb (volleyball without hitting, just catching and throwing). I never heard another complaint from the young lady and often caught her smiling during games. Previous classes had involved skills that were above her ability level—she felt she could not contribute to the team and she was frustrated. Now she was able to help the team, she was developing a sense of belonging, and she felt she could safely risk attempting a bump because she could go back to catching if things didn't work out. The activity was now providing her with a sense of social and emotional safety.

Social and emotional development are so tightly connected that they are presented here as one topic, unlike the cognitive and physical. Meeting a social need often has a direct emotional effect and vice versa. Meeting social and emotional needs may well be the key to promoting physical activity. If physical activity does not connect with a child's social and emotional development, present as well as future participation are threatened.

We are social beings. We all have a need for social contact, and children are no exception. Emotionally, we need to feel competent. What better tool is there for meeting these needs than playing a game?

Many researchers have studied the social and emotional development of children. Teaching children social skills such as helping others, cooperating, listening, being empathetic, and respecting the rights of others is important. This social responsibility cannot develop until children are given the opportunity to make decisions (Hellison 2003). A nonthreatening environment is conducive to learning and positive social and emotional development. If the learning environment requires children to perform at a level above their ability, the result is frustration. If the task is below their ability, boredom ensues.

Children who can make good decisions, persevere, motivate themselves, and maintain hope in the face of frustration are more successful than those who cannot (Goleman 1995). Allowing children to select their level of participation, share ideas, communicate, collaborate, and negotiate provides opportunities for real decision making while creating an atmosphere where players are more likely to persevere.

Activities in this book offer social experiences that allow children to

- work together,
- express themselves,
- help others and be helped,
- create rules,
- negotiate, and
- cooperate.

Children will not feel comfortable in these social situations unless the atmosphere is emotionally safe. For example, children don't feel safe when there is not enough action and too many eyes are focused on one player's mistakes. To create an emotionally and socially safe environment, players should feel that they belong to the group because they can make contributions. For all players to be able to contribute, the leader must allow for multiple levels of skill and offer appropriate choices for each. These social objectives meet NASPE standards 5 and 6 (see appendix A).

Cognitive Needs

Let's turn to the cognitive development of children. Don't worry—in this book, cognitive development involves no sitting behind a desk, no rulers to measure the circumference of a basketball court, and no trivial questions such as "Run the number of laps that represents the number of sides in a triangle." Paper, pencils, books, and computers are not required. Our cognitive developmental tool is movement. It is time to dispel the myth that when the body engages, the mind disengages.

Adult organized, adult run, adult coached—this is the description of many children's programs, including dance, music, sport, and recreation. Children need opportunities to think for themselves. As the leaders of these "children's programs," we need to step back and give the children some of the decision making. In Carry On (page 114), the players decide their individual roles and the team plans its own strategies. Mission Impossible (Almost) (page 76) allows children to discuss, try, evaluate, and try again. These are just two examples of activities where adults can assign positions and teach the answer. However, if we are interested in cognitive development, we need to facilitate an environment in which children can learn by doing, and not teach or coach the answer.

Effective cognitive learning depends on providing the correct challenge level. According to Caine and Caine (2003), self-efficacy, or perceiving one's ability as effective, often comes from decision making (cognitive skills) within a safe environment. In addition, self-efficacy is a major factor in determining future participation in physical activity.

The activities in this book do not focus on memorizing a list of facts and figures, information that in many cases children will never need again unless they are involved in a serious game of Trivial Pursuit. Instead, games in this book provide opportunities for

- planning strategies,
- analyzing and evaluating plans, and
- generating alternative solutions.

To help children develop these cognitive skills, the leader must create an atmosphere of social and emotional safety. For cognitive development to continue, children need to be able to choose from a spectrum of choices in each activity. After conquering a group initiative (chapter 6), if a team has to repeat the same problem over and over until time is up, they will most likely become bored. Since the group has solved the problem, they should be allowed to move up to the next level of difficulty, challenging themselves and maintaining a high motivational state. On the other hand, in Baseball or Kickball (page 92), a player can make the decision to move down a level and attempt to hit a self-pitched ball. In addition to enhancing physical skill, such choices provide an emotional sense of belonging because the players can choose the level where they can best contribute to the team effort.

Let's examine physical development next. This book focuses on the use of games as opposed to "exercise." But don't be fooled—the players will get plenty of exercise, just in a different form.

Physical Needs

"Are we done yet?" A nine-year-old wanted to know if his class was finished with their run. "No. You haven't even run for two minutes yet," was my reply. At that point in my career I felt that the kids were complaining because they were out of shape. What I failed to realize was that most of the kids were in shape, but the activity—jogging laps—was not meeting their needs. It wasn't that these children didn't want to run because of poor conditioning, but because I was using an inappropriate adult model of exercise on them.

Now my students run longer and harder than before. They don't perceive running as work, something boring, or something that must be done first before they can have fun. Why? Because instead of mindlessly running laps, the running is part of a game we play, a game designed to meet students' needs. The same concept applies to skill development. Waiting in line to practice a skill is boring and an ineffective use of time, and it can be a source of negative social and emotional pressure. Playing a well-designed game can meet your skill objective, lighten the mood, and increase the time on task.

Children have a need for physical fitness, including

- aerobic fitness,
- flexibility, and
- muscular strength and endurance.

They also have a need for physical skills, including

- eye–hand–object coordination,
- motor planning,
- static and dynamic balance, and
- object manipulation.

This section focuses on how to meet these needs. Keep in mind that children are different and need programs designed with those differences in mind.

According to the Council of Physical Education for Children (COPEC), children's physical activities should not be "watered down adult or sport activity" (1992, p. 4). COPEC has also stated that exercise guidelines are based on research of adults and are not appropriate for children (1998). Jogging laps, calisthenics, and weight training are all adult forms of exercise, and when they are substituted for well-planned and designed games, the movement experience or perception changes from one of play or fun to work.

Several studies indicate that children are underactive. However, the problem with most of these studies is that they use an adult definition of physical activity—periods of sustained movement. Children are not continuous movers. Children move sporadically all day long. When you add up the number of active minutes, children are the most active segment of the American population (Blair et al. 1989).

Recognizing the difference between children and adults, NASPE (1998) recommends that the greatest portion of children's physical activity comes from lifestyle activity. NASPE defines lifestyle activity for children ages 5 to 12 as "active play and games involving the large muscles of the body" (p. 10). Aerobic exercise for this age group would include games that are moderate to vigorous and that follow an intermittent pattern, alternating periods of exercise and brief rest. (See table 1.1 for a report on the heart rates of children during active play.)

Physiological Factors Specific to Children

Physiologically, children are not the same as adults.

1. Maximum heart rate does not decline until after puberty (Bar-Or 1983); therefore the traditional target heart-rate formula is inappropriate for children because the formula assumes a decline in maximum heart rate with age.

2. Children have a larger ratio of surface area to body mass, which means in hot environments they gain more heat than adults and in cold environments they lose more heat than adults.

3. Sweat output is lower for children. This means children have less evaporative cooling in addition to their greater heat load in hot environments.

4. Children are metabolically inefficient compared to adults—running at the same speed as an adult costs the child more energy.

Table 1.1   Heart Rate Values

Game	Average heart rate	Number of students
Hoop Tag	176.04	28
Foot Fencing	163.71	28
Dee Fence	163.85	26
Where'd They Go?	166.79	19
Capture the Flag	168.39	62
Around the World Basketball	155.63	9

Active play such as tumbling, climbing, and stunts is appropriate for promoting flexibility for children ages 5 to 12 (NASPE 1998). Formal flexibility exercises are not necessary. Games that allow children to push, pull, lift their own weight, and otherwise use their muscles a bit harder than normal promote muscular strength and endurance. Clearly, traditional calisthenic exercises and laps are not the only way to promote physical fitness and activity.

Let's not stop here. In our efforts to improve fitness we sometimes neglect skill. This book promotes the development of skill by using simple games as opposed to lines and drills. Instead of teaching every single sport, which would be impossible, the games in this book work on skills inherent in many sporting activities, such as visual tracking, throwing, catching, striking, determining angle of projection, absorbing force, and so on. Skill opens the door to increased participation and social interaction.

The games in this book could easily be described as the active play and games that NASPE recommends, and they generally meet NASPE standards 1 through 6 (see appendix A). However, this book goes well beyond the NASPE recommendation by equally addressing children's social, emotional, and cognitive needs all in the same game.

Now that we have taken a look at whole-child teaching and the social, emotional, cognitive, and physical needs of children, let's turn to the concepts behind the games and activities in this book.

Designing Games for the Whole Child

When you understand the concepts that were used in developing the games for this book, you can create and adapt new activities. Often you will find a new game that has a few problems, making it incompatible with teaching the whole child. To modify such games, it helps to have an idea of what games for the whole child require. We'll begin with a concept called equalization.

Competition As a Motivator

Many physical educators, recreation leaders, camp counselors, and before- and after-school supervisors believe that competition is necessary to motivate children. Competition is a hot topic, and many would place themselves in either the competition or cooperation camp. I belong to both camps. I do not believe that competition is necessarily harmful, nor do I believe it is necessarily motivational. I do believe that competition's ability to motivate depends largely on the structure of the competition.

Children can compete in a wide variety of activities, from a soccer game to a simple activity like Tire Tug (page 85). If children are involved in a steady stream of competitive experiences in which they are on the losing end of a lopsided score, they may become frustrated and turned off to the activity. Those who repeatedly trounce their opponents can become bored and turned off to the activity as well. In either case, competition is not necessarily motivational, and it can have an immediate or long-term consequence that no physical educator wants—turning kids off to physical activity.

In most cases, the problem is that the children are not being challenged at their ability level. Now hold on! I am not going to suggest that the players be separated into different games according to ability. Within the same game, children need to be challenged at the appropriate level. This challenge according to ability is known as equalization (Torbert 1996).

Equalization

Equalization (Torbert 1996) is a concept used in designing games that can help a game meet a child's needs. Equalization means allowing players to participate at their own level. This usually requires having several options available to all students because ability levels vary greatly even among children of the same age. Players can develop a sense of competence and a sense of belonging, and they become more willing to risk an attempt at the next higher skill level.

An example of equalization can be found in the game of Baseball or Kickball (page 92). In this game a child may choose to hit a pitched ball or a ball from the batting tee. All players are free to choose up or down the range of skills. In a game of Grass Hockey (page 96), equalization is accomplished when a team that is two points ahead of the opponent has their challenge increased by the other team. The team that is behind institutes the challenge, such as doubling the size of the winning team's goal (challenging their defensive abilities) or reducing the size of their own goal (challenging the shooting ability of the winning team). As soon as the two-point deficit is down to one point, the equalization rule is removed.

Equalization will not result in perfect, everybody's-happy scores at the end of the game. However, it does usually result in closer scores, and it challenges children at a level more appropriate for their ability. Children who are challenged at their own level will increase their sense of self-competence, or self-efficacy. Children who perceive themselves as physically competent are more likely to remain active throughout their lives. When children are allowed to participate at their own level and when they witness others participating at different levels, they begin to understand that we are all unique. Understanding and respecting differences is the first step to understanding and respecting others. This is part of NASPE standard 5—respecting self and others in physical activities.

"What Have I Done?"

Some fifth graders were playing a cooperative version of volleyball called Infinity. In this game, the players on both sides of the net are part of the same team. Points are scored for each successful volley over the net. If the ball touches the floor the group must start over and try to beat their previous best.

One group was happily involved in the game, with some children bumping and setting the ball while others were catching and throwing it. They had made cognitive choices appropriate for their individual level of play (equalization). They were not practicing for a skill test, but playing for the joy that challenging oneself at one's own level can bring.

At that point, Mr. Know-It-All (that was me) went over to the group and asked if they had heard that Mrs. Volleymaster's (not her real name) class had hit the ball over the net 25 times. Could they beat Mrs. Volleymaster's class record? Children who had been happily bumping and setting were now throwing and catching. They were no longer challenging themselves at their own level. What had I done?

I changed the focus from fun to comparison with others. I'm guessing that children who were bumping and setting did not want to be blamed for a mistake and not beating the other class. So they began to catch and throw. In retrospect, my actions said that I did not have confidence in the activity to motivate the children.

I've since learned my lesson. When children enter an activity that enables them to choose their level of participation and also offers plenty of action (expansion, or lots of turns to do something), they don't need outside motivation. I no longer keep class records or challenge students to beat another class. It simply is not necessary and sometimes even has the effect of lowering skill development.

Other Game Factors

Equalization is just one concept in game design. Other important concepts include

- eliminating elimination,
- maintaining plenty of action,
- having ample equipment, and
- negotiating problems.

Eliminating players causes social and emotional harm. It also reduces time spent practicing, so we need to eliminate the use of elimination. Elimination is often subtle. A tagged player who must do 10 push-ups to reenter a game has been eliminated, even if just temporarily.

One way to increase the action of a game is to have smaller teams. A game with 22 players and one ball is developmentally inappropriate and causes the bunching you often see in youth soccer.

Having ample equipment increases action, allows more practice time, and means players aren't standing in line waiting for a turn. When was the last time you saw children lining up for their turn to read the social studies book? If your budget is small, it may be necessary to make some equipment, such as hula hoops from PVC pipe and tennis rackets from coat hangers and panty hose.

Negotiation means allowing children to solve problems themselves. In order for this to occur, the game leader must remove the referee shirt. Players involved in a conflict should be removed from the game and allowed to correct the situation. During negotiation, players should follow these guidelines:

- Speak one at a time.
- Listen to each other.
- Agree on a solution.
- Report the solution to the game leader.

Once this is accomplished, the players return to the game.

As you move on to the games, refer often to appendix A. This appendix will tell you about the developmental needs each game addresses. Remember that the objective is teaching the whole child—the social, emotional, cognitive, and physical—through games.

Now let's play!

Warm-Up Games

A warm-up prepares the body for more intense exercise. A warm-up should gradually increase the heart rate, muscle blood flow, and body temperature to the levels required by the more intense exercise. Prepubescent children will elevate their heart rate and plateau faster than adults, so warming up is not as crucial for children as it is for adults. The games in this chapter are designed to get children who have been sitting in a classroom moving through light exercise, which takes the form of simple games.

Little Bit of This, Little Bit of That

Indoor or outdoor

| 3 | 1, 2 | 1 | 1, 2, 3, 4 |

NASPE 1, 2, 5, 6

Equipment

- A music source such as a CD or tape player and fast, upbeat music appropriate for the age group
- Other equipment depends on the variation; see How to Play

Play Space

40 × 60 feet (12 × 18 meters)

Setup

Have the music source ready. Put any equipment (such as balls) in boxes on the sidelines around the playing area to avoid pushing and shoving as players reach for equipment.

How to Play

Players perform an action when the music is on and another action when the music is off. For example, when the music is playing, the players get a basketball and dribble (right-handed, left-handed, alternating) around the room without touching anyone else. When the music stops, they all shoot their ball. When the music comes back on, they dribble again. Or, they might dribble a volleyball when the music is on and serve, bump, or set to the wall when the music is off.

Strategies for Success

- When a player is attempting a basket, all the basketballs go up and then come down, occasionally on someone's nose. This causes some players a bit of anxiety. I am fortunate to have five basketball goals. I put out several racks of basketballs and a box of softer, lighter volleyball trainers. Children who choose the volleyballs are given designated baskets to shoot at. They may still get hit in the head, but not nearly as hard.

- Take advantage of teachable moments, briefly stopping the action and reviewing skills such as underhand serves or dribbling control.
- To create an atmosphere of trust and security, offer challenges such as dribbling with only the right or left hand, alternating.
- Try using foam or regular soccer balls on an outdoor field.

Hustle Hoops

Indoor or outdoor

1, 2, 3   **1, 5**   **1, 2**   **2, 3, 4, 5**

NASPE 1, 2, 5, 6

Equipment

- Enough hoops for 2 players per hoop (a dozen hoops for a group of 24)
- A music source such as a CD or tape player and music with a fast tempo

Play Space

40 × 60 feet (12 × 18 meters)

Setup

Randomly spread the hoops around the playing area. Have the music source ready.

How to Play

At the start of the music, players move through the playing area without stepping inside the hoops. When the music stops, players get into the hoops as fast as possible. Time the group to see how quickly they can get in. Players may share hoops. In each successive round, remove one hoop and start the music again.

Strategies for Success

- To prevent hoops from becoming overcrowded, allow players to place only one foot inside.
- Watch out for the last child to get in a hoop. Keep the other children from blaming the last child for not setting a new record. As the leader you can manipulate your counting (slow it down, speed it up, and so on).
- Playing until there is only one hoop left can lead to pushing and shoving, the opposite of a helping environment. With 28 players I usually stop when there are about five hoops remaining.

- Have players dribble a ball during the music, stop dribbling when the music stops, and get in a hoop. I have seen children hold balls overhead so that players can fit in—this is creative, but don't coach it.

Adapted, by permission, from M. Torbert, 2001, *Follow Me: A handbook of movement activities for children.* Pages 18-21 and 160. Available from P.L.A.Y. Resource Center, 4274, Boulder Ridge Pt., Eagan, MN., 55122-1899. (651-687-9062), PLAYCENTER@aol.com.

Limbo Rock

Indoor or outdoor

1   5   9   5, 6, 7

NASPE 1, 2, 5, 6

Equipment

- The "Limbo Rock" song (most party cassettes and CDs contain this song)
- A CD or tape player

Play Space

40 × 60 feet (12 × 18 meters)

Setup

Have the music ready. Divide the players into groups of six or so (odd numbers are okay). Space groups evenly throughout the playing area.

How to Play

Part 1

Dancers line up side by side, a few inches apart. They stand with their feet together. All groups face the leader and do the following movements.

Counts

  1   Right toe touches out to the side
  2   Right toe touches in next to the left foot
  3   Repeat count 1
  4   Repeat count 2

After count 4, repeat, but on the left

  5   Left toe touches out to side
  6   Left toe touches in next to right foot
  7   Repeat 5
  8   Repeat 6

Part 2

Keeping both feet together, dancers do the following movements.

Counts

9	Swivel heels to the right
10	Swivel toes to the right
11	Repeat count 9
12	Repeat count 10
13	Swivel toes to the left
14	Swivel heels to the left
15	Repeat count 13
16	Repeat count 14

Part 3

Keeping both feet together, dancers do the following movements.

Counts

17	Jump back and clap
18	Repeat count 17
19	Repeat count 17
20	Repeat count 17

Part 4

The dancers at the end of the lines walk forward on a diagonal to meet. The two dancers form an arch with their arms. The other dancers then walk single file under the arch, limbo fashion (head tipped back, chest out with arms to the sides). Dancers do not have to go under the arch in any particular order.

Dancers then reform their line and repeat the dance beginning with count 1. The next arch is formed by the next two dancers from each end of the line, and so on.

Strategies for Success

- Don't dance for perfection; keep the structure loose.
- It helps for the leader to verbalize the movements. For example, the leader can shout out, "Out, together, out, together!" or "Toes, heels, toes, heels!" and so on.
- Practice several rounds without music.

Bring Back My Body

Indoor or outdoor

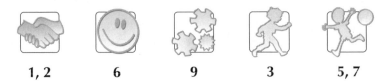

| 1, 2 | 6 | 9 | 3 | 5, 7 |

NASPE 2, 3, 4, 5, 6

Equipment

A willing voice, not necessarily a good one

Play Space

8 × 20 feet (3 × 6 meters)

Setup

Have players sit on gymnasium bleachers, classroom chairs, picnic-table benches (facing out), or whatever is available.

How to Play

Sing the following to the tune of "My Bonnie Lies Over the Ocean":

> My body lies upon the sofa
> My body sees too much TV
> My body eats junk food and pizza
> Oh, bring back my body to me
> Bring back
> Bring back
> Bring back my body to me, to me
> Bring back
> Bring back
> Bring back my body to me

As the song begins, have the players stand the first time they hear the word "body" and sit the next time they heard the word "body." This continues for the rest of the song.

Strategies for Success

- Caution players not to sit on the edge of their chairs, as they may slip.
- Increase the challenge and fun by having children stand and sit on all words beginning with a "B."
- Get creative, be silly, have fun. Without telling the kids it's coming, I've added, "My body sees too much 'Beavis and Butthead,'" or "Bring back my body to Ben and Bob (Brian Barrett, Betty Boop, and so on)." The children usually laugh at their silly teacher and have fun while warming up.
- If your players are ready, begin with half the group standing and the other half sitting. This creates an alternating standing and sitting routine. Players will need to focus on the sounds and not let the contradictory visual input distract them.

Towelball

Indoor or outdoor

2, 4, 9   **1, 2**   **2, 3, 5, 6, 8**   **2, 3**   **8, 9, 10, 11**

NASPE 1, 2, 3, 4, 5, 6

Equipment

- 1 old towel for each set of partners
- 1 beanbag for every 2 players

Play Space

40 × 60 feet (12 × 18 meters)

Setup

Group players into pairs and give each pair a towel and a beanbag.

How to Play

Players begin by using the towel to toss a beanbag about 6 feet off the towel and then catch it with the towel. Challenge players to see how many consecutive catches they can make. A drop means the pair starts again, attempting to beat their previous best. Increase the height challenge as each pair is ready.

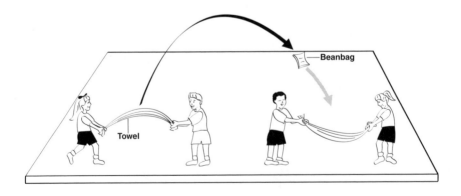

Strategies for Success

- Using a blanket or bed sheet increases the difficulty. I have found it much harder for children to coordinate when there are six players as opposed to just two. However, have the challenge available for those groups who are ready.
- Quite often I end up with a group of three players. Try having two players hold the towel while the third player tosses the beanbag high into the air to the towel players. The towel players then toss the beanbag to the third player. Have the players rotate positions every 10 attempts.
- Change the challenge by having a group of two toss the beanbag to another group.
- Have players toss for distance or height.

Egg Beater

Indoor or outdoor

1, 2, 10   **5**   **6, 9**   **3**   **6, 9**

NASPE 1, 2, 3, 4, 5, 6

Equipment

1 long jump rope

Play Space

40 × 60 feet (12 × 18 meters)

Setup

Have players form a single-file line.

How to Play

The leader turns a long rope with a volunteer or ties the other end of the rope to a game standard, tree, or fence. As the leader turns the rope, the first player in line simply runs through the rope, not stopping to jump it. On each successive turn of the rope the next player runs through the rope. If the rope comes around and a player does not run or is hit by the rope and the rope cannot be recovered, stop and then restart.

In round 2 have the players go through with a partner. They don't have to hold hands, but they do have to go at the same time. In round 3 players go through in threes and in round 4 they go in fours. Each round will cause the players to increase their speed. In round 1, players can walk to get back in line. In round 2 they will walk fast or jog slowly. By rounds 3 and 4 they will be running.

Strategies for Success

- Challenge the group to get as many players as they can through the rope before a miss. If a player misses, allow that player the opportunity to restart.
- As the leader, if you are turning the rope (I recommend you do), you can assist those having trouble by speeding up, slowing down, increasing the rope's arc, and so on.
- Playing for more than 5 to 8 minutes turns the activity into a cardio workout.

Think About It

A traditional version of this warm-up would be to have the children walk a lap or two, then fast walk a lap, and then jog a lap or two. The Egg Beater better meets the needs of children than the traditional version.

Skill Practice

The activities in this chapter make practicing skills a playful experience. Gone are the children lined up behind cones, waiting in line for their turn to hit the ball. Because everyone is active, there is much less focus on any one child's particular failure. These activities take the drudgery out of traditional skill drills.

Bottle Blast

Indoor or outdoor

1, 2   **1, 5**   **3, 4, 5**   **1, 9, 10, 11, 12,**
13, 16, 20, 24

Equipment

- 2 or 3 volleyball nets (or more)
- As many volleyball trainers (larger and lighter than regular volley-balls), beach balls, or lightweight foam balls as possible (ideally 1 per player)
- 15 to 25 1-liter seltzer bottles, 2-liter soda bottles, or plastic bowling pins per team
- Floor tape or two long ropes

Play Space

40 × 60 feet (12 × 18 meters)

Setup

Arrange the volleyball nets so they divide the play space into two halves. Divide players into two teams, and place one team on each side of the net. Place 15 to 25 soda bottles behind each team. Using floor tape if inside or a rope if outside, create a restraining line a few feet in front of the bottles. Players may not stand behind the restraining line to block a ball. Give half of the available balls to each team.

How to Play

On your signal, players begin hitting the balls over the net, trying to knock down the opposing team's bottles. When defending the bottles, players may not go behind their restraining line. Players must try to catch the balls coming over the net, not hit them. Once a player retrieves a ball, that player may hit the ball over the net in an attempt to knock down the other team's bottles.

Strategies for Success

- This game can be chaotic, so make sure the balls are lightweight.
- Allow players to make a return without catching when trying the bump and set, if they choose.
- Players are allowed to retrieve balls that have gone behind the restraining line and stopped rolling, but they must leave the area as soon as possible.
- Play different rounds practicing the underhand serve, overhand serve, forearm bump (pass), and overhead set.

Think About It

One of the important aspects of this book's games is equalization, or playing at one's level of ability. In Bottle Blast, players are free to choose how close or how far away from the net they would like to practice. Contrast this to the traditional strategy, where players line up behind cones and all practice from the same distance. How might the traditional strategy affect a child's perception of competence?

Botkey

(BOTtle-hocKEY)

Indoor or outdoor

1, 2   **1, 5**   **3, 4, 5**   **2, 3**   **1, 9, 13, 14,
                                                                    15, 16**

NASPE 1, 2, 3, 4, 5, 6

Equipment

- 1 Dom Ringette stick per player (bladeless hockey stick; available from Flaghouse at www.flaghouse.com)
- 2 carpet squares per player
- 1 beanbag or Super-Safe Puck per player (available from Sportime at www.sportime.com)
- Empty seltzer or 2-liter soda bottles, enough for 10 or 12 bottles per team

Play Space

40 × 60 feet (12 × 18 meters)

Setup

Divide players into two equal teams. Place each team behind opposite side-lines of a basketball court. Halfway in between both teams, place a line of seltzer or soda bottles parallel to the sideline players. Bottles should be two different colors—for example, green (lemon-lime) and red (cherry), or any other color as long as there are two (color is determined by the flavor of the soda or a piece of colored tape placed around the bottle). Alternate bottle colors. Each player places a carpet square under each foot and gets one ringette stick. Pass the beanbags out to each team.

How to Play

On your signal players shoot the beanbags in an attempt to knock down their team's soda bottles. Each team aims at their team's color. If the wrong bottle is knocked over, it stays down.

Strategies for Success

- No slap shots allowed. To shoot the puck, players place their stick on the beanbag, draw it backward, and then slide it forward.
- Put two players from each team out in front of the sideline and the bottles. These players do not stand on carpets. Their job is to shoot stopped beanbags back to their teammates.
- Try the game outside with foam soccer balls and cones of two different colors. Players do not stand on carpets, and there are no players in the middle to retrieve balls. Call a time-out when necessary to allow players to get balls from the center and return to the kicking line.

Think About It

A phrase found in this book is "focus off failure." In Botkey, so many players are active at once, there is no one standing around watching other players miss shots. How might keeping players from focusing on a failed attempt affect their perseverance?

Boxball

Indoor or outdoor

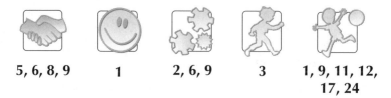

5, 6, 8, 9   **1**   **2, 6, 9**   **3**   **1, 9, 11, 12, 17, 24**

NASPE 1, 2, 3, 4, 5, 6

Equipment

1 8-inch (20-centimeter) bouncing ball for each group of players

Play Space

10 × 10 feet (3 × 3 meters) for each group of players

Setup

Divide players into groups of four. Using floor tape if inside or driveway chalk if outside, create a box that is 10 × 10 feet (3 × 3 meters), divided into quarters. Make a box for each group of players. Mark the quarters 1, 2, 3, and ACE. Give each team one ball.

How to Play

The player in the ACE square begins the game by serving the ball to square 1, 2, or 3. For a serve to be legal, the ACE must drop the ball and let it bounce one time, then hit the ball underhand. The player in box 1, 2, or 3 returns the ball by hitting it with either hand before the ball bounces twice in their square. Violations include hitting the ball into your own square; letting the ball bounce twice in your square; hitting the ball out of bounds; catching the ball; carrying the ball; and throwing the ball. A player who commits a violation moves to box 1 and all other players move up. If player 3 hits the ball out of bounds, he goes to square 1, player 1 goes to square 2, player 2 goes to square 3, and the ACE player remains where he is. The only way the ACE gets out is if the ACE makes a mistake (misses a shot, hits the ball out of bounds, or commits a violation of the rules).

Strategies for Success

- Do not allow the serve rule or catching rule to be changed; they prevent any unfair advantage.
- The kids are quite capable of making the rules for their game. Some teams may allow spiking (a crushing overhand hit), while others may not. Some may allow bobbling (almost like a catch but the players keep tapping the ball with their hands so that they do not actually catch the ball). Creating rules and abiding by them are important social skills.
- If the group does not divide nicely into teams of four, play several games with teams of five or six (more than that and the wait time would be too long). In this setup, the player making a mistake should go out of bounds to a waiting line and switch with the player waiting to play. The waiting player should go to box 1 while all other players rotate as usual. An alternative might be to create a court shaped like a pizza instead of a square. Each player would stand in one slice. Designate slice 6 as the ACE and slice 1 as the slice players go to when they make an error.

Think About It

Children are interested in action. Do not be surprised if you see a child hit the ball out of bounds and the next player goes ahead and hits the ball. Adults might immediately shout, "The ball is out." But children who are more interested in action will keep playing the ball. It is not that they don't understand; they simply view the game differently. Let them play on.

Geography Dodgeball

Indoor

1, 2, 4

1, 5

2, 3, 8

**1, 6, 10, 13,
18, 20, 24**

NASPE 1, 2, 5, 6

Equipment

- As many soft foam balls as possible (1 per player)
- Cones or floor tape
- 2 large laminated maps (one map of the United States and one world map)
- 2 playground or therapy balls in different colors, 24 or 36 inches (61 or 91 centimeters) in diameter

Play Space

40 × 60 feet (12 × 18 meters)

Setup

Tape the maps to the wall. Divide the class into two teams and give each team half of the foam balls. Place the two large colored balls in the middle of the room. Each team should be about 20 feet (6 meters) from the middle, facing each other. Tape a restraining line in front of each team. Three feet (1 meter) in front of each team's restraining line, tape a scoring line.

How to Play

Assign each team one of the colored balls as their target ball. Players throw the foam balls at their target ball. When the target ball crosses the scoring line of the other team, a point is scored. The team that didn't score goes to the map and has 10 seconds to locate a specific spot (state, country, river, ocean, and so on). If that team is successful they also score a point. Place the large balls back in the center and start again.

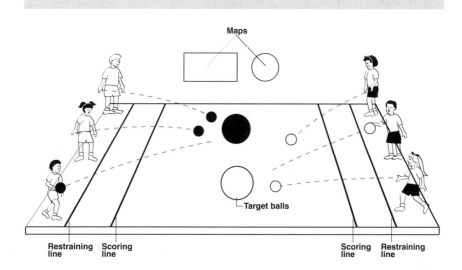

Maps

Target balls

Restraining   Scoring
line   line

Scoring   Restraining
line   line

Strategies for Success

- One or two players from each team should be allowed to stay in the center with the target balls to throw balls back to their teammates. These players are not allowed to interfere with shots.
- Designate one player from each team as the official map "pointer." This player does not have to find the location, but her finger should be the only one on the map when the count of 10 is up.
- Players may make defensive throws to move the opposing team's target ball away from the scoring line.
- Purchase a large ball printed like a globe, which becomes the only target ball. Both teams throw at the globe.

Globetrotters

Indoor or outdoor

1, 2, 4, 9   **1**   **2, 9**   **1, 9, 10, 13,
                                                         17, 20, 21, 24**

NASPE 1, 2, 5, 6

Equipment

Several bouncing balls for each group of players

Play Space

40 × 60 feet (12 × 18 meters)

Setup

Divide players into groups of five or six. Spread the groups throughout the playing area. Each group forms a circle, standing slightly farther apart than hand-holding distance.

How to Play

The first player gets the ball and passes to any player in the group. After passing, player 1 kneels to signify that he is done. Player 2 receives the ball, passes to any of the standing players, and then kneels. This continues until the last player receives the ball. The last player passes the ball to player 1. The group has now established their pattern, and all players must continue to pass the ball to the player they originally passed to.

Strategies for Success

- Play "Sweet Georgia Brown" (the Harlem Globetrotters' theme song) in the background to add to the fun.
- When the group is ready, they may add a second, third, or even fourth ball so that multiple balls are being passed around the circle at the same time.
- As balls are added to the circle, emphasize that if some players make bounce passes while other make chest passes there will be fewer midair collisions.

- Have several types of balls available for each group, including basketballs, volleyball trainers (larger and lighter than regular volleyballs), fleece balls, and large foam balls (some balls will not be good for bounce passes). This helps create emotional safety, as some players don't like the idea of getting hit with the harder balls.

Adapted, by permission, from M. Torbert, 2001, *Follow me: A handbook of movement activities for children.* Pages 18-21 and 160. Available from P.L.A.Y. Resource Center, 4274, Boulder Ridge Pt., Eagan, MN., 55122-1899. (651-687-9062), PLAYCENTER@aol.com.

Hose Tennis

Indoor

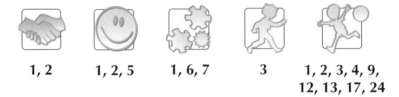

1, 2   1, 2, 5   1, 6, 7   3   1, 2, 3, 4, 9,
                                                           12, 13, 17, 24

NASPE 1, 2, 3, 4, 5, 6

Equipment

- 1 panty-hose tennis racket for each player
- 1 balloon for every player

Play Space

40 × 60 feet (12 × 18 meters)

Setup

Make panty-hose tennis rackets according to the instructions in appendix B (page 145). Place rackets and balloons around the perimeter of the playing area. Players select a racket and balloon and spread out.

How to Play

Give the players different challenges:

- How many times in a row can each player hit the balloon up in the air without the balloon hitting the ground?
- Alternating the faces of the racket, how many times can each player hit the balloon without letting it touch the ground?
- Walking around the room using forehand and backhand strokes, how many times can players hit the balloon so that it does not touch the ground?

Strategies for Success

- The larger the balloon, the more it floats and the easier it is to hit. Under-inflated balloons travel faster and are a more appropriate challenge for players who are ready. Have a variety of balloon sizes available for the players to choose from.

- When ready, players can pair up. Have one partner put her balloon away, leaving one balloon for the two players. The players are then challenged to volley as many times as possible before the balloon touches the ground. Each player may hit the balloon only once in succession.

Think About It

Many teachers may feel tempted to find the child who has the most hits to motivate the class. This is unnecessary, however, because the focus is on each player bettering a previous performance. What effect can focusing on the "winner" have for those who never win?

Hot Shots

Indoor or outdoor

1, 2, 10   **1, 2**   **1, 3, 9**   **1, 3**   **1, 2, 3, 4, 8, 9, 11, 13, 16, 24**

NASPE 1, 2, 3, 4, 5, 6

Equipment

- As many soft throwing objects (foam balls, yarn balls, fleece balls) as possible
- 1 pillow case–sized bag for each team

Play Space

40 × 60 feet (12 × 18 meters)

Setup

Place four teams at one end of the playing area. At the same end, spread the balls on the floor. Each team sends two players to the opposite end of the playing area to hold their team's bag or "basket" open. Designate areas from which a made shot is worth three points, two points, or one point, with more points earned for shots from a greater distance.

How to Play

On your signal, all players pick up one ball and shoot for their team's basket. Players must retrieve a missed shot before getting the next ball. Missed shots can be picked up and shot from that spot. All players shoot at the same time. The players holding the basket may move to try to assist their team members, but they may not release the basket and use their hands to help. Play until almost all the balls are gone. Stop and restart the game with new basket holders for each team.

Strategies for Success

- Players can keep track of their own points.
- Consider placing a net (tennis, volleyball, badminton, and so on) at an appropriate height in front of the shooting area to increase the likelihood of a more arched shot.

Sling It

Outdoor

1, 2, 10, 11 **1, 2, 5** **4, 5** **10, 11**

NASPE 1, 2, 5, 6

Equipment

- 1 water-balloon slingshot for each group of 6 players
- As many beanbags or dense foam balls as possible
- Cones

Play Space

50 × 200 feet (15 × 61 meters)

Setup

Play outdoors on a large field. Divide your group into equal teams of about six players. Four players from each team begin the game as shooters and take a position behind the designated starting line. The remaining two players take hold of the slingshot. Every 20 feet (6 meters) from the starting line, place a cone until you have five scoring zones. Each shooter gets two shots.

How to Play

On your signal all teams may shoot, but no one may retrieve until your signal (when all shooters are finished). On your signal all teams retrieve their objects. An object that lands somewhere in the first zone, 0 to 20 feet (0 to 6 meters), scores one point; an object that lands in the second zone scores two points; and so on. All players gather the beanbags or balls and add the points. Rotate within teams to have two different players become slingshot holders and shooters for each round.

Strategies for Success

- Never allow players to aim the object at other players.
- Each team's projected objects should be identifiable. Using different-colored objects for each team makes counting the score much easier.

- Even though the players are counting points, there is no need to announce one team as the winner.
- Use grass paint or cones to create a target with concentric rings that are 15 to 20 feet (5 to 6 meters) wide. Award points based on the ring in which the object lands. Vary the points per ring so that an outer ring is worth more than an inner ring or the bull's-eye. This helps children develop a sense of force.

Give 'n' Go

Outdoor

2, 3   1, 2, 5   1, 6, 9   1, 3   1, 2, 3, 4, 6, 8,
9, 10, 11, 13,
18, 19, 21, 24

NASPE 1, 2, 3, 4, 5, 6

Equipment

- 1 soft football for every 2 players
- 4 cones or markers

Play Space

50 × 50 feet (15 × 15 meters)

Setup

Set up a large outdoor square, placing cones at the corners. Have the students line up evenly around the square, standing shoulder to shoulder, facing the interior of the square. Have the students count off, numbering as a One or a Two. Ones become quarterbacks and get the ball for the first round, while Twos will play receivers during the first round. Players will switch roles for every subsequent round (Ones become receivers and Twos become quarterbacks, and so on). When it is time to switch, students should return to their original starting position before play resumes so that the players are back in an evenly dispersed formation.

How to Play

On your signal all receivers run toward a quarterback on a different side of the square. The quarterbacks remain on the sideline, looking for receivers. When a receiver gets a quarterback's attention, the quarterback throws the ball. A catch results in a point for both the receiver and the quarterback. Receivers return the ball to the quarterback by handing the ball off. Receivers then run to another quarterback who is standing on a different side of the square from the side they just came from. Have the players switch roles after 1 minute.

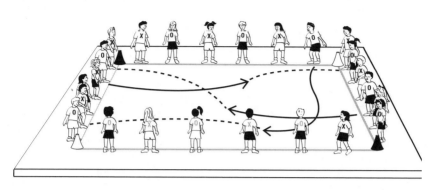

X = Quarterback O = Receiver	Solid line = Run path of receiver.	Dashed line = Flight path of QB's pass.	X's stay on sideline while O's run for passes.

Strategies for Success

- Play third and fourth rounds in which the quarterbacks face away from the inside of the square and receivers run across the square, tap a quarterback on the shoulder, and run away for the pass. The quarterback should attempt to lead the receiver for the completed pass.

- Another strategy for setting up this activity is to divide the group into partners, who should stand next to each other in the square. The game is played the same way, with the receivers seeking out different quarterbacks. When it is time for players to switch roles, it is easy to tell them to go back to their original partners and switch jobs.

Fitness Games

The fitness games in this chapter do not include any traditional exercises. Doing sit-ups in a hula hoop is not fun just because a hula hoop is involved, and calisthenics are not fun simply because they are called *fun*damentals. Instead, this chapter includes games that allow children to intermittently run and rest while developing aerobic fitness. Pushing and pulling activities help to develop muscular strength and endurance, while games that move the joints through a large range of motion promote flexibility.

All Tied Up

Indoor or outdoor

1, 2, 4, 9   **1, 5**   **2, 4, 5, 7**   **5**

NASPE 2, 3, 4, 5, 6

Equipment

Deck tennis rings, tube socks, or strips of cloth

Play Space

40 × 60 feet (12 × 18 meters)

Setup

Divide players into groups of five or six. Give each player one strip of cloth. Have the players stand in a circle and reach into the center with both hands. Players grab another player's piece of cloth with their free hand. Make sure that any two players do not grab only each other's cloth strip; each player should be connected with two different players.

How to Play

Once the players are "all tied up," the challenge is to become untied, ending up in a circle where they are all connected by the cloth strip to the player next to them. Some players may end up facing out of the circle, which is acceptable as long as the group is in a circle.

Strategies for Success

- Having players hold a piece of cloth or deck tennis ring eliminates the sometimes awkward hand-holding issue and can help prevent wrist injuries.
- Discourage the students from beginning by holding the cloth strip of the player immediately to the left or right.

- Allow players to release the cloth if they feel their arm or wrist is being twisted. They should regrasp the cloth without any other advantage.

Bleachers and Bench

Indoor or outdoor

| 1, 3 | 1, 2, 5 | 1, 3, 9 | 1, 3 | 1, 2, 3, 4, 5, 10, 15, 23 |

NASPE 1, 2, 3, 4, 5, 6

Equipment

1 bouncing ball for each player

Play Space

40 × 60 feet (12 × 18 meters)

Setup

Have all players spread out randomly on one side of a rectangular or square playing area (a basketball court works well). The players must be behind the line on that particular side of the court, or the "bench." The opposite side of the playing area is the "bleachers." Give each player a ball.

How to Play

If the leader shouts, "Bleachers," the players dribble toward the bleachers side of the playing area. If the leader shouts, "Bench," the players dribble toward the bench side. If a player has not made it all the way to the side when the next call is made, the player simply turns around and dribbles in the direction of the new call. When the leader shouts, "Time-out," all players get down on one knee and tuck the ball under an arm. Play several rounds. Increase the difficulty by designating one of the remaining sides as the baseline and the other as the three-pointer.

Strategies for Success

- Try the game outside using soccer balls.
- Additional commands increase the challenge:
  - "Injury" (Players assume a supine position, place the ball on the belly, and yell, "OHHH!")

- "Around the world" (Players stop dribbling and start passing the ball around their waist in a circular fashion.)
- "Globetrotters" (Players find a partner and pass both balls back and forth, one using a chest pass, the other a bounce pass.)

Bottle Rockets

Indoor or outdoor

1, 2, 3   **1, 2, 5**   **1, 2, 4, 5**   **1, 3**   **1, 2, 3, 4, 8, 9, 16, 18, 24**

NASPE 1, 2, 3, 4, 5, 6

Equipment

- 4 large tumbling mats or cardboard refrigerator boxes (make sure there are no protruding staples)
- 1 soft throwing object per player

Play Space

40 × 60 feet (12 × 18 meters)

Setup

Stand a box or tumbling mat in each of the four corners of the playing area. The tumbling mats should form a cylinder. Divide the players into four teams of equal size and assign them a box. Place one or two players from each team inside their box. Spread the balls on the floor.

How to Play

On your signal, the players outside the box begin picking up the balls and throwing them into the boxes of the other three teams. They also defend their team's box, trying to keep out the other team's balls. The players inside the boxes throw the balls out as quickly as possible. At your signal, all action halts. The team with the fewest balls in their box wins. Pick new players to go in the boxes and start again.

Strategies for Success

Consider using cones or tape to mark a circular stay-out zone around the boxes to keep players from crashing into the boxes.

Capture the Flag

Outdoor

| 1, 2, 4, 5,
8, 9, 10, 11 | 1, 2, 5, 8 | 1, 2, 3, 4,
5, 6, 7, 9 | 1, 3 | 2, 3, 4,
15, 21 |

NASPE 1, 2, 3, 4, 5, 6

Equipment

- 37 cones
- 36 beanbags
- 12 hoops
- Cloth flags (in 3 different colors)

Note: You'll need a cloth flag for every player, so if there are 8 players on the red team, 8 players on the blue team, and 8 players on the yellow team, you would need 8 red flags, 8 blue flags, and 8 yellow flags. I often have the players were color-coordinated pinnies so that their team affiliation is obvious.

Play Space

Circle with 100-foot (30-meter) radius

Setup

Divide players into three teams, with each team member wearing an identifying flag at the waist. Form a center circle with 12 cones. The diameter of the circle should be 20 to 30 feet (6 to 9 meters). Place one cone in the center of the circle. Using nine cones, create three lines spreading out from the outer edge of the center circle so you have what looks like a large pizza with three slices. Each slice is a given team's home zone. In the center of each team's home field and about 60 feet (18 meters) from the center circle, make another circle of 5 cones with a diameter of about 15 feet (5 meters) and place a container holding a dozen beanbags in the center. Finally, randomly scatter four hula hoops in each team's home zone.

How to Play

On your signal, the game begins. The objective is for players to successfully enter another team's zone, capture a beanbag, and return safely to their home zone. All players are safe from being tagged while in their home zone or while inside the large center circle. A player may capture only one beanbag at a time. If tagged, a player must go to jail. Going to jail simply means that the tagged player goes to the center circle, touches the cone in the middle, and is then free to play. If a player is tagged while escaping with a beanbag, she must return the beanbag and then go to jail.

Any player from an opposing team can find temporary safety by standing in a hula hoop in one of the other team's zones. Only one player per hoop is allowed (you can modify this), there is no time limit, and the home-team players may choose to guard their hula hoops. Home-team players may set up a defensive perimeter around their supply of beanbags, but they are not allowed inside to tag an opposing player. The only time a home-team player is allowed inside the circle containing his beanbag box is when depositing a captured beanbag from an opposing team. If a player fleeing with a beanbag enters another zone and is tagged, the tagged player deposits the beanbag in the tagging team's box before going to jail.

Strategies for Success

- Periodically stop the game and have the players return to their home zone to count the beanbags. Allow 30 seconds to a minute for each team to discuss their team strategy.
- Allow each team to decide what their roles (offensive or defensive) will be. Don't assign the positions.

- When players cannot agree if one was tagged, move the players to the sideline and allow them to settle the dispute. When it is settled, they should report their decision to the leader before reentering the game. Some suggestions from the instructor may be helpful in resolving this situation.

- Consider allowing the third-place team to borrow a player of their choice from the team in first place, a form of equalization called a complimentary handicap (Torbert 1996). This means that the third-place team now has an extra player and the first-place team will be challenged because they have lost one of their best players. It is not an exchange of players.

Think About It

In the original version of the game, each team had one flag. Quite often the fastest player from each team was the only one to ever have a chance to capture the flag. Can you determine which game design concepts (see chapter 1) are enhanced with the multiple-flag modification? The original version also had tagged players go to jail and wait to be rescued before playing again. Is the center jail cone consistent with proper game design (chapter 1)? Is it still a subtle form of elimination or a focus on failure? How does not having a jail and the associated consequence of temporary elimination lead to more players taking risks and trying to capture a flag?

The Chicken and the Coyote

Indoor or outdoor

1, 2   **1, 6**   **1, 9**   **1, 3, 4**

NASPE 2, 3, 4, 5, 6

Equipment

- 1 rubber chicken
- 1 stuffed toy coyote

Actually, any 2 objects are fine—just change the name.

Play Space

40 × 60 feet (12 × 18 meters)

Setup

Line the players up shoulder to shoulder on one side of the playing rectangle. Give the first player in line the rubber chicken.

How to Play

On your signal, player 1 passes the chicken to player 2, who passes it to player 3, and so on. As each player passes the chicken, she turns and runs behind the other players and gets in line at the other end. Players continue to pass the chicken and reform the line around the rectangle until the chicken has made a complete lap of the playing field. Time the group so that in subsequent rounds the team can be challenged to beat their best time.

In round 3 add the coyote. After player 1 passes the chicken, have him wait until the chicken reaches the fifth player and then give player 1 the coyote. As soon as he passes the coyote, he can go to the end of the line. Stop the time when the chicken and coyote have returned to the start.

Strategies for Success

- Allow players to pass each other as they run behind the line.
- Have players lie on their backs for round 2. Players pass the chicken, get up, run to the end, and lie back down. In my experience this version works best—there is more order and less chaos as the players run to the end of the line.

Cone Tipping

(No Cows Needed)

Indoor or outdoor

1, 2   1, 2, 5, 6   1, 3, 5, 7   1, 3   2, 3, 4,
                                                    15, 21

NASPE 1, 2, 3, 4, 5, 6

Equipment

1 cone for every player

Play Space

40 × 60 feet (12 × 18 meters)

Setup

Give each player a cone and scatter the players around the playing area. Ask half of the players to knock their cone down.

How to Play

On the leader's signal, all the players next to a standing cone must move around the area and stand up any cone that is lying down. All players who began the game with a cone that was knocked over must try to knock over as many cones as they can.

Strategies for Success

- In round 1, allow the players to use only their hands to knock over and pick up the cones, but in subsequent rounds you can allow them to use different body parts (feet, knees, elbows, only thumbs, and so on).
- Have players reverse roles after several rounds.

Adapted, by permission, from C. Hinson, 1995, *Fitness for children* (Champaign, IL: Human Kinetics), 70.

French Fries and Frankfurters

Indoor or outdoor

1

1, 5, 8

1, 3, 9

1, 3

**2, 3, 4, 5,
15, 21, 23**

NASPE 1, 2, 3, 4, 5, 6

Equipment

12 cones

Play Space

40 × 60 feet (12 × 18 meters)

Setup

Divide players into two equal teams. One team is the frenchfries and the other is the frankfurters. Players form two parallel lines facing each other in the center of the playing field. Using three or four cones, create a safety line 20 to 30 feet (6 to 9 meters) behind each group. The location of the safety line depends on the space you have to work with, but 30 feet is the maximum for a larger space.

How to Play

The leader calls either "French Fry" or "Frankfurter." The team that is called chases the other team. The team being chased must quickly turn and run for safety behind their safety line. Once behind this safety line, players may not be pursued. The chasers tag as many players as they can. Tagged players become members of the chasing team. When all chased players are behind their safety line, the leader should call all players to the middle and restart the game. Begin each call with "Frrrrrrr. . ." to build the suspense. Start the next "Frrrrrr. . ." before all players have returned to the starting position.

Strategies for Success

- Do not place safety lines too close to a wall; keeping the line at a safe distance prevents players from running into the wall.
- Do not eliminate tagged players so as to designate a class champion.
- Use other words that begin the same, such as "Drrriver and Drrragon," "Crrrane and Crrrow," or "Trrrain and Trrruck."

Think About It

When I first began using this game years ago, I would wait for the last player to return to his side in the middle before starting the next round. Occasionally I would even say, "Come on Johnny, we're all waiting" (focusing on failure). I eventually discovered that if I simply began the next "Frrrr," the players would automatically hustle back to their starting line, turning the game into a cardio workout.

Dee Fence

Indoor or outdoor

| 1, 2, 12 | 1, 2, 4, 5, 6 | 1, 2, 3, 6, 8, 9 | 1, 3 | 2, 3, 15 |

NASPE 1, 2, 3, 4, 5, 6

Equipment

Tube socks, strips of cloth, or flags

Play Space

40 × 60 feet (12 × 18 meters)

Setup

Divide players into teams of 4, 5, or 6. Each player on the team except one takes a flag. The players with a flag make a circle facing inward and hold hands, forming the fence. The fence players hang a flag from the back of their shirt collar (if they have long hair they can tuck the flag in the back of their waistband). The player without a flag should stand outside the fence and will attempt to steal the flags. Set some boundaries for each group so that teams do not share the same play space—each team plays in their own zone.

How to Play

On the signal to begin, the odd player outside of the circle attempts to take as many flags as possible. This player cannot grab the fence players or reach through the circle. Fence players are not allowed to let go of hands, but they may move as a group to the right or left in a circular motion. At the conclusion of the round, select another player to take the flags.

Foot Fencing

Indoor or outdoor

3, 5, 7   **1, 4**   **1, 9**   **1, 3**   **2, 3,**
                                                          4, 15

NASPE 1, 2, 3, 4, 5, 6

Equipment

2 pieces of foam pipe insulation for every 3 players, about 3 feet (1 meter) long

Play Space

40 × 60 feet (12 × 18 meters)

Setup

Divide players into groups of three and give each group two fencing foils (the insulation). Spread the groups throughout the playing area and designate a separate playing area for each—groups should not overlap.

How to Play

In round 1, two players fence and the third is the referee. At the leader's signal, each fencer tries to hit the opposing player's foot. Fencers should move to avoid having their foot hit. Referees keep score, making sure players stay in the designated area. Each round lasts 30 to 45 seconds. At the conclusion of the round the referee fences the winner. No player may fence more than two consecutive rounds. Players should keep their nonfencing hand on their forehead to guard against any cranial collisions.

Strategies for Success

- A similar game uses hollow plastic tubes or rolled newspapers, but my experience has shown these to be somewhat intimidating and therefore socially and emotionally unsafe.
- Swinging the fencing foil too high or wildly is a common problem that the game leader must carefully watch for.

- Occasionally, when you set up groups of three, you will have one player left over (if you have a class made up of 25 students, for example). In this case, have one group of four players. With these four players, have players 1 and 2 fence each other while players 3 and 4 fence each other at the same time—no referees. If two players are left over (if you have a class made up of 26 students, for example) they fence each other. When it is time to rotate, they would rotate one player between a designated group of three. Rotate as follows: 1 versus 2 and 3 versus 4, then 1 versus 3 and 2 versus 4, then 1 versus 4 and 2 versus 3.

The Good, the Bad, and the Healthy

Indoor or outdoor

1, 2, 3   **1, 5**   **1, 2, 3, 8**   **1, 3**   **2, 3, 4,
15, 21**

NASPE 1, 2, 3, 4, 5, 6

Equipment

- 4 hula hoops
- 20 or more beanbags
- 20 or more yarn balls

Play Space

40 × 60 feet (12 × 18 meters)

Setup

Place a hula hoop in each corner of the playing area. Place five beanbags and five yarn balls in each hoop. Divide the players into four teams of equal size and place one in each corner.

How to Play

On your signal, each player runs to another team and takes one beanbag, depositing the beanbag in their own team's hoop. Players may also take one yarn ball from their own hoop and deposit it in another team's hoop. At the conclusion of the game the team with the most beanbags and the least yarn balls wins.

Strategies for Success

- Players may not guard their hoop or interfere with other players.
- To reinforce health concepts that may be covered in a classroom lesson, have the beanbags represent good cholesterol (HDL) and the yarn balls represent bad cholesterol (LDL). Active lifestyles promote the development of higher levels of good cholesterol.

Think About It

If players were allowed to give or take more than one object at a time, what effect would it have on the remaining players? Would it reduce or increase the amount of action (expansion) available to all players?

Adapted, by permission, from S. Virgilio, 1997, *Fitness education for children* (Champaign, IL: Human Kinetics), 174.

Where'd They Go?

Indoor

1, 3, 5   **1, 2, 3,**   **1, 6, 9**   **1, 3**   **2, 4, 6, 9, 13,**
              4, 8   **18, 20, 24**

NASPE 1, 2, 3, 4, 5, 6

Equipment

- 4 folding gymnastics tumbling mats, 5 × 12 feet (1.5 × 3.5 meters), or 4 large cardboard boxes
- Cones
- Soft foam balls

Play Space

40 × 60 feet (12 × 18 meters)

Setup

Divide the players into two teams. Stand one mat like an accordion in each of the four sides of the playing area, leaving enough room for players to safely run behind the mats—if the mats are too close to a wall or some other obstacle, serious collisions may result.In the center of the playing area, use cones to mark a circle with a diameter of 10 feet (3 meters).

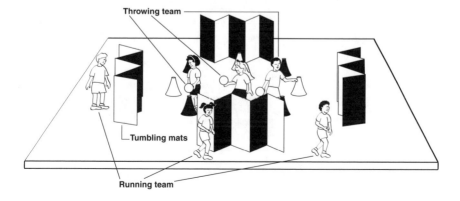

Throwing team

Tumbling mats

Running team

How to Play

Team 1 runs around the perimeter of the gym in one direction only. Team 2 is in the center of the gym within the circle of cones. Team 2 throws soft foam balls at the players from team 1, who may hide behind the mats. Players hit by a ball are not out; they simply continue running. Hits to the head do not count and must be discouraged. Teams switch roles after every minute.

Strategies for Success

- *Never* use any ball that could cause injury. Some foam balls have a covering or coating that prolongs their life span but also causes a stinging hit. Use uncoated foam balls or yarn balls.
- Do not put a time limit on how long players may stay behind the mat.
- Throwers may leave the throwing area when they need more balls, but they may not throw until they return to the center circle.
- Throwers earn a point for each player they hit (except for hits to the head, which don't count). Runners score a point each time they reach the next mat. If players are hit on the way to the next mat, they do not score a point. After three hits, players must start over counting points in an attempt to beat their previous score. It is up to the players to keep their score if they choose.

Think About It

In the original game players switch roles every 2 minutes. Any player hit by a ball is eliminated and sent to the sidelines for the remainder of the period. How do the game's modifications enhance the game physically and emotionally? In the original version, players are limited to 5 seconds of hiding before they have to leave. How might this affect risk taking and how might it affect a player emotionally?

Adapted, by permission, from E. Foster, K. Hartinger, and K. Smith, 1992, *Fitness fun* (Champaign, IL: Human Kinetics), 85.

Hoop Tag

Indoor

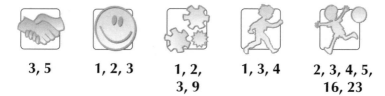

3, 5   **1, 2, 3**   **1, 2,**   **1, 3, 4**   **2, 3, 4, 5,**
                          3, 9   **16, 23**

NASPE 1, 2, 3, 4, 5, 6

Equipment

1 hula hoop per child (4 different colors)

Play Space

40 × 60 feet (12 × 18 meters)

Setup

Play on a smooth surface, such as a tiled cafeteria floor or wood gymnasium floor. Have players spread out, each standing inside a hoop.

How to Play

Announce one hoop color as It. On your signal, all players in that color of hoop chase the other players and try to tag them. A tagged player trades hoops with the tagger and becomes It. There are no tag-backs, a term I learned from my students that means when you tag me and we trade hoops I can't immediately tag you—I have to wait at least 10 seconds. Players move hoops by shuffling their feet. Both feet must stay in the hoop. Players may not pick up hoops with their hands.

Strategies for Success

- If you notice several players off to the sidelines, don't argue or tell them they must play or else! Simply call their color as It and they will automatically become active. Children want action. Not enough action sends the message that the game is not challenging enough.

- To reduce hard tagging, give all It players a foam ball for tagging players. Players simply hand off the ball when tagged.

Hoop Passing

Indoor or outdoor

1, 2, 4, 9   **1, 2, 5, 6**   **2, 3, 4, 5, 7**   **5**

NASPE 2, 3, 4, 5, 6

Equipment

As many hula hoops as possible

Play Space

40 × 30 feet (12 × 9 meters)

Setup

Divide the children into teams of 6, 7, or 8. Players stand side by side holding hands (or strips of cloth if hand holding is an issue). Divide the hoops evenly between the teams, stacking the hoops on the floor next to each team's first player.

How to Play

On your signal, the first player from each team picks up one hoop, steps through it, and passes it over her head, down her arm, and on to the next player. Players must not let go of hands. The first player then reaches for the next hoop, not waiting for the first hoop to reach the end of the line. When the last player has passed through the hoop, he drops it on the floor at the end of the line. When all hoops are at the end of the line, the last player picks up a hoop and reverses the process. Play for 1 minute.

Strategies for Success

- If players let go of hands, the leader takes one hoop back to the start.
- If a team begins with six hoops and all six make it to the end in the allotted time, the team scores six points. If all six make it to the end and two come back to the start, the team scores eight points, and so on. The goal for each team is to improve their previous high score.

- If you make your own hoops from PVC plumbing pipes, which are stronger than store-bought hula hoops and much less expensive, try making different sizes. Smaller hoops are more challenging.
- Young players can stand side by side without holding hands. They simply step through the hoop and hand it to the next player in line. Teachers at the Monmouth Day Care Center in Red Bank, New Jersey came up with this modification.

Show Me the Money!

Indoor or outdoor

3   1, 2, 3, 4   1, 9   1, 3   2, 3, 4, 5

NASPE 1, 2, 3, 4, 5, 6

Equipment

- 1 soft foam ball for each player
- A source of music, such as a CD or tape player

Play Space

40 × 60 feet (12 × 18 meters)

Setup

Using a permanent marker, number the balls consecutively. Write corresponding numbers on pieces of paper and put them into a hat or bowl. Give one ball to each player and have the players scatter throughout the playing area.

How to Play

When the music starts the players move around the area using various locomotor patterns—walk, skip, gallop, run, shuffle, slide, and so on (leader may choose). The leader stops the music, which signals the players to stop, and pulls six numbers from the hat. All players with a ball matching a winning number are It. Those who lost drop their ball and flee from the winners, who keep their ball. The winners tag the nonwinners with their ball, scoring $1,000,000 for each player tagged. Play for 30 to 45 seconds. As the music begins again, all nonwinners pick up a new ball. Winners may keep their ball or exchange it for another. All players move around the area using a new locomotor pattern. When ready, the leader puts the winning numbers back in the hat and draws another six numbers.

Strategies for Success

- The music period may also be used as an opportunity for players to walk and catch their breath, consistent with children's natural sporadic movement patterns.
- If gambling and the lottery are controversial in your community, simply change the name of the game and the dollar concept.

May I?

Indoor or outdoor

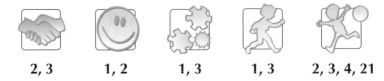

2, 3   1, 2   1, 3   1, 3   2, 3, 4, 21

NASPE 1, 2, 3, 4, 5, 6

Equipment

- 1 tube sock, flag, or cloth strip per player
- 6 hula hoops

Play Space

40 × 60 feet (12 × 18 meters)

Setup

Randomly scatter the hoops around the playing area. All players tuck a flag in the back of their shirt collar, or if they have long hair, in their waistband. Players spread out.

How to Play

Each player attempts to steal as many flags as possible while maintaining possession of his flag. When a player steals a flag, he keeps it in hand and does not place it in his waistband or throw it on the ground. If a player loses his flag, his remaining job is to simply steal flags—he is not eliminated. A player being chased can enter a hoop and be safe. Players may not guard the hoops, and there is no time limit on how long a player can stay in a hoop. Only one player at a time is allowed in a hoop. A player must leave the hoop if another player with a flag approaches, tags her, and says, "May I?" If all six hoops are occupied by the final six players to have flags and none are leaving the safety of the hoops, you can designate a signal that means all players have to leave and find another hoop, or you can start another game and declare those six the winners.

Strategies for Success

The hula hoops provide a place for a quick rest, consistent with children's intermittent activity pattern, and they offer players an emotional safety outlet.

Think About It

How would eliminating players whose flags are stolen affect their ability and their willingness to take risks?

Mission Impossible (Almost)

Indoor or outdoor

2, 4, 9, 10, 13   **1, 6**   **2, 3, 4, 5, 7**   **5**

NASPE 1, 2, 3, 4, 5, 6

Equipment

1 rope, 5 feet (about 1.5 meters) long, for each player

Play Space

40 × 60 feet (12 × 18 meters)

Setup

Divide the players into pairs. Tie a slip knot at both ends of each rope. Place each end of the rope around each wrist of the first player. Slide the knots up, but keep it comfortable. Place one end of the second rope on one wrist of the second player. Loop the second rope through or behind the first player's rope and then tie the loose end onto the second player's other wrist. The two ropes now connect the players.

How to Play

Players attempt to free themselves from their partner without untying the knots or removing the rope from their wrists

Strategies for Success

- Monitor players for any unsafe use of the ropes. Do not allow players to pull or twist ropes in an unsafe manner.
- Allow partners to remove the ropes and begin again if they find themselves in a dangerous position, such as when a rope is around someone's head.
- This is a fun activity, but keep it short. The important part of the game is the process, not the product, which is truly difficult.

- When players claim they have solved the problem, I have them do it again while I watch. More often than not they broke a rule in their first attempt. When they free themselves again in my presence, I can point out mistakes or confirm their victory.

Number Chase

Indoor or outdoor

1, 2, 3, 5   **1, 2, 8**   **1, 3, 8, 9**   **3**   **2, 3, 4, 15, 21**

NASPE 1, 2, 3, 4, 5, 6

Equipment

- 1 large pair of dice (available at www.sportime.com or www.flaghouse.com, or can be made from cardboard)
- Cones, enough to mark the safe zone

Play Space

40 × 60 feet (12 × 18 meters)

Setup

Divide players into two groups. Participants face off on opposing lines about 3 feet (1 meter) apart. One group is the odd team and the other is the even team. Use cones to mark a safe zone about 20 feet (6 meters) behind each team.

How to Play

The leader begins the game by rolling one die down the middle of the two teams. If the die comes up on an even number, players on the odd team turn in the opposite direction and players on the even team chase them. Any player on the odd team who is tagged before reaching the safety zone becomes a member of the even team. The reverse is true when an odd number is rolled.

Strategies for Success

- Make sure players don't have to run and then stop at a boundary that is close to a wall. Allow plenty of space for slowing down.
- To increase physical activity, don't wait for all players to return to the center. Simply hold the die over your head and say, "Here we go, what will it be, odd or even?" Players will scramble to get back for the next round.

- Increase the challenge by throwing both dice and having the players
  - add the numbers,
  - subtract the smaller number from the larger, or
  - multiply the numbers.
- For younger players, cover the faces of the dice with different colors (red versus green), letters (a-b-c versus x-y-z), shapes (squares versus triangles), or simple numerals (1-2-3 versus 7-8-9).

Pivot-Pass-Pop

Indoor or outdoor

1, 2, 5   **2, 3**   **1, 6, 8, 9**   **1, 3**   **1, 2, 3, 4, 8, 9,
15, 16, 18, 19,
20, 21, 24**

NASPE 1, 2, 3, 4, 5, 6

Equipment

1 soft foam ball for each group of 3 players

Play Space

40 × 60 feet (12 × 18 meters)

Setup

Write a different number on each ball so that players do not pick up the wrong team's ball and cause an argument. Form groups of three players and give each group a ball.

How to Play

Each group decides who is It, the player who will run from the other two. The two players try to hit the It player with the ball. The player with the ball may not travel, but she may pivot to pass or throw at the runner. The player with the ball may travel after they have made a pass or throw. When the runner is hit, the team regroups and a different player is the runner. The runner gets a 3-second head start.

Strategies for Success

- This activity uses human targets. Never use any ball that could cause physical or emotional injury. I believe coated foam balls are unacceptable for throwing at another person. I use the least expensive, lowest density uncoated foam balls I can find.

- Here is an alternative version that my students enjoy:
  - Form groups of four players and give each group a ball. Spread groups throughout the playing area. Each group divides into pairs and decides who will be the first team to be chased.
  - The chasing players try to hit either of the running players. As before, the player with the ball may not travel but may pivot to pass or throw at the runners. When a runner is hit, the teams switch roles.

Push-Up Hockey

Indoor

| 5 | 1, 2 | 2, 6 | 2 | 9, 13 |

NASPE 1, 2, 3, 4, 5, 6

Equipment

1 beanbag for each pair of players

Play Space

40 × 60 feet (12 × 18 meters)

Setup

Divide players into pairs. If there is an odd number you can have a group of three. Partners face each other about 10 feet (3 meters) apart. Both players assume a modified or regular push-up position. Give one of the players a beanbag.

How to Play

The player with the beanbag attempts to slide (no throws allowed) the beanbag between the hands of his partner for a goal. The defending player may block the beanbag with her hands, but she may not drop down to her elbows or belly. When a shot goes wide, the defending player retrieves the beanbag and takes her turn.

Strategies for Success

If you have a group of three players, use a triangle formation. The players slide the beanbag in order around the triangle.

Scrambled Eggs

Indoor or outdoor

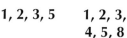

1, 2, 3, 5   **1, 2, 3,**   **1, 3, 4, 5**   **1, 3**   **2, 3, 4,**
              4, 5, 8   **15, 21**

NASPE 1, 2, 3, 4, 5, 6

Equipment

- A music source, such as a tape or CD player
- 4 hula hoops
- 6, 7, or 8 soft tagging objects such as foam balls (depending on team size), yellow if possible

Play Space

40 × 60 feet (12 × 18 meters)

Setup

Divide the group into four teams of 6, 7, or 8 players. Scatter the hula hoops around the playing area. Have each team select a name. Determine which team is It and give each player on that team a soft object to tag members of the other teams.

How to Play

Each It player receives a point for every player tagged. Players who are It may not tag a player with at least one foot in a hoop, and they may not guard the hoops. The players being chased may stay in a hoop as long as they want. Once players leave a hoop they may not return until they have gone to another hoop. They score a point for every hoop they run to without being tagged.

Briefly stop the music and call the next team It. The previous It players drop the tagging objects and begin running to hoops with the other two teams. Players accumulate points from one round to the next, but when tagged for a third time, they lose all points and start over, trying to beat their personal record. Repeat enough times that all teams are It at least once.

Strategies for Success

- Why scrambled eggs? Use the game to discuss a health concept. The hoops are the egg whites, the healthiest part of the egg. When players get to the hoop, they get a point for avoiding too many yolks (foam balls).
- It is up to the players to count points. Make no reference to how many points anyone has scored.

Think About It

The hoops give the players a chance to take a break, which is consistent with children's natural sporadic movement pattern. What effect does providing hoops and not eliminating tagged players have on a player's willingness to take risks?

Tire Tug

Indoor or outdoor

1, 2, 10, 12   **1, 2**   **2, 3**   **2, 3**

NASPE 2, 3, 4, 5, 6

Equipment

- 8 plastic soda bottles (2-liter) or cones
- 1 soft cotton rope, 2.5 inches (6 centimeters) in diameter and 9 feet (2.74 meters) in length
- 4 tumbling mats, 5 × 12 feet (1.5 × 3.5 meters)

Play Space

30 × 40 feet (9 × 12 meters) for each game

Setup

In the center of two side-by-side tumbling mats, form a circle, or the tire, with the rope. Tie two ends of the rope with a square knot. The diameter of this rope circle should be about 3 feet (1 meter). Divide the players into four teams and have each team sit around the mat, about 10 feet (3 meters) away from the corners. Each team sits to the side of their bottle. The players on each team number off from 1 to 4.

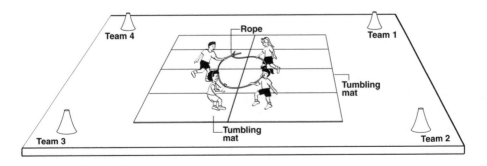

How to Play

The leader calls a number, and the player with that number from each team walks to the center of the mat. All four players lift the rope and the leader signals to begin the contest. The players attempt to pull the rope toward their own team. When a player is close enough to his cone, he lets go of the rope with one hand and knocks down the cone for two points. If no one has won after about 30 seconds, stop the contest and award a point to each team for the tie. Call out the next number and begin the next contest. Play two games simultaneously to increase involvement.

Strategies for Success

- In the past, this game was played with a bicycle tire covered with foam pipe insulation and duct tape. This is no longer recommended, as wire within the tire can poke through the insulation and tape, causing hand injuries.
- Encourage a player who falls not to let go of the rope, as this usually results in the other three players falling.
- End the round if a player cannot get up.

Think About It

To add a cognitive element, ask the players who lost if there is anything they could do to win if they met up in another contest with the player who just won.

Four-Way Tug

Outdoor

**1, 2,   1, 2, 5   2, 3   2, 3   5, 23
10, 13**

NASPE 1, 2, 3, 4, 5, 6

Equipment

- 1 four-way tug-of-war rope
- 4 different-colored cones

Play Space

100 × 100 feet (30 × 30 meters)

Setup

Divide the players into four groups of about the same size. Stretch the rope out in a north, south, east, west orientation. Place a cone about 8 feet (2.5 meters) from each end of the rope. Assign each group one end of the rope. The players may lift the rope but may not pull until you give the signal.

How to Play

On your signal, all players pull the rope in the direction of their team's cone. When the last player of a team is close enough to the cone, she lets go of the rope with one hand and knocks the cone down. Mix up teams for each round.

Strategies for Success

- Teams score two points for a win and one point for a tie. End rounds after a minute. Let the players briefly rest between rounds.
- If a team looks as if they are getting close, you can shout, "Look out for the orange (color of their cone) team!" This may cause the other teams to form a temporary alliance to stop that team, and it adds listening skills to the game.

5

Sport Games

The games in this chapter are modified versions of popular sporting activities. These versions offer more action, fitness, and choices not to mention more fun for children of different abilities. Modifications include smaller teams, more equipment, and several rule changes. Imagine how much more time players spend on task with five soccer balls in a game or three players on a football team, or how the choice between hitting off a batting tee or a pitched ball in baseball not only improves skill but also adds a whole new emotional dimension.

Around the World Basketball

Indoor or outdoor

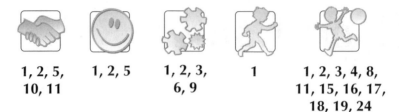

1, 2, 5, 1, 2, 5 1, 2, 3, 1 1, 2, 3, 4, 8,
10, 11 6, 9 11, 15, 16, 17,
18, 19, 24

NASPE 1, 2, 3, 4, 5, 6

Equipment

Each team should receive one of the following (in that team's colors where possible):

- Basket
- Ball
- Cone
- 4 flags

Play Space

40 × 60 feet (12 × 18 meters)

Setup

Divide the class into five groups of four or six players. Each group divides in half into offense and defense. Place a cone beneath and behind each team's basket. Place each team's flags in the top of their cone and give each team the ball that matches the color of their flags.

How to Play

On your signal, all offensive players dribble and pass the ball in the direction of an opposing basket. Teams must make a minimum of two passes before any player can shoot. When a basket is made, a player from the offensive team takes one of the defensive team's flags and moves on to the next basket. If the offense misses and rebounds, they must make two passes before the next attempt. If the defensive team rebounds the ball, they hand the ball over to the offensive team, who must leave and attempt a basket at another goal. If the defensive team that rebounded the ball is the only team left that the offense needs a flag from, then the offense must shoot and hit their own backboard

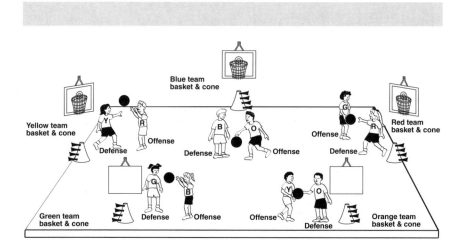

before making another attempt. The first team to capture a flag from each of the other teams wins. Have players reverse roles for round 2, and in round 3 rotate a few players from every team and begin again.

Strategies for Success

There may be a lot of double dribbling, traveling, and up and downs, even a few fouls. Take some time, perhaps 30 seconds in between rounds, to discuss concepts such as traveling, double dribbling, and carrying the ball. However, don't let these rules interfere with the game's action, which is what the kids are interested in.

Baseball or Kickball

Outdoor

1, 2, 5, 7   **1**   **2, 3**   **1, 6, 8, 9, 10,
                                                   11, 12, 13, 14,
                                                   18, 19, 20, 24**

NASPE 1, 2, 5, 6

Equipment

- Batting tee or 30-inch (76-centimeter) cone
- Wiffle-ball bats
- 1 Wiffle ball
- 1 foam kickball
- 3 carpet squares

Play Space

50 feet (15 meters) from home base to first and from home to third base.

Setup

Divide the players into groups of 4, 6, or 8 depending on which version you are playing (1 versus 3, 3 versus 3, or 4 versus 4). Use the batting tee as home base and carpet squares as first, second, and third bases. One player is the batter or kicker and the others are fielders. Each player has the option of hitting or kicking. Players who hit may choose to hit from the tee or pitcher, or they may self-pitch. Kicking choices are place kicking, punting, and kicking a rolled pitch.

If possible, offer bats in three different sizes (thin stickball, regular, and wide fungo).

How to Play

1 versus 3

When a player hits or kicks the ball, she must attempt to get to as many bases as possible. Runners are not allowed to stop at a base, so they must keep going until they are all the way around or tagged out. Fielders must tag a runner out except at first base, where the fielder can touch the base with the ball in hand to get the runner out. Runners score a point for each base touched. When fly balls are caught, the player is out and no runs are scored. Fielders may not try to hit the runner with the ball for an out. After the runner is out, she rotates into the field and a new player is up to bat.

3 versus 3 or 4 versus 4

In these versions the runner may stop at a base. There is no leading off, stealing, or tagging up. All players bat twice (not in succession) and then they switch with the fielders, even if there are no outs. Runners stranded on base return the next inning.

Strategies for Success

With 3 versus 3 use only home base, first, and third bases. This avoids the use of ghost runners, which can be confusing.

Think About It

In a typical game of softball or kickball where half the class plays the other half, most players are lucky to have one opportunity to hit or kick the ball. Infielders might have several chances to catch and throw, but outfielders might not. Contrast the traditional game to this version.

Bottle-Cap Football

Outdoor

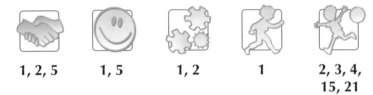

| 1, 2, 5 | 1, 5 | 1, 2 | 1 | 2, 3, 4, 15, 21 |

NASPE 1, 2, 3, 4, 5, 6

Equipment

- 1 plastic bottle cap or other small object
- 2 tube socks, flags, or cloth strips for each player

Play Space

65 ×150 feet (20 × 46 meters)

Setup

Divide the group into two teams of equal size. All players tuck a tube sock in their waistband on each of their sides. One team starts as offense and the other as defense.

How to Play

The offensive team huddles with the leader, and one player is given the bottle cap. All offensive players make a fist, turn to face the defense, and act as if they each have the bottle cap. On the leader's signal ("Hike"), all offensive players begin running toward their goal line as if they each are going to score a touchdown. Defensive players must find the offensive player with the bottle cap by pulling a sock from as many players as they can. If an offensive player has a sock removed, he must show the defensive player his hands. If the offensive player with the bottle cap is found, the team begins their next play from that location. The offensive team has four chances to score a touchdown before the players switch roles.

Strategies for Success

- Once the players get the hang of the game, play two games simultaneously.
- Designate one player from each team to hand out the bottle cap. You might want to have a brief discussion about who gets the bottle cap. The bottle cap doesn't have to alternate between boys and girls— this is too easy for the defense to figure out—but rotation should be fair.

Grass Hockey

Outdoor

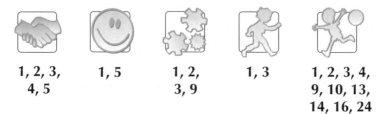

1, 2, 3,   **1, 5**   **1, 2,**   **1, 3**   **1, 2, 3, 4,**
4, 5   **3, 9**   **9, 10, 13,**
                                           14, 16, 24

NASPE 1, 2, 3, 4, 5, 6

Equipment

- 4 cones
- 1 plastic hockey stick for each player (different colors for different teams)
- 2 Wiffle balls for each game

Play Space

40 × 60 feet (12 × 18 meters) per game

Setup

Divide the players into teams of two offensive players and two defensive players (four total). Each team has sticks in the same color and a matching ball—using two balls greatly increases the action and spreads it throughout the field. Each team places their cones in a line about four strides apart to form a goal.

How to Play

The game begins with each team's offensive players facing each other in two parallel lines about 10 feet (3 meters) apart. On the signal, one player from each team hits their ball toward the other team. Each team tries to shoot their ball into the opposing goal; teams cannot score in their own goal. Teams face off after each goal. Each team's offensive and defensive players change positions with every goal scored. High sticking is anything above the waist.

Strategies for Success

- If a team gets two points ahead, the team that is behind institutes a challenge rule. For example, they may decide that the opposing team must double the size of their goal (increasing the winning team's defensive challenge), or that they will decrease the size of their own goal by 50 percent (increasing the winning team's offensive challenge). The losing team can also borrow a player of their choice from the winning team. The challenge rule ends as soon as the deficit is less than two points.

- If a team is four points ahead the game is over. Teams change several players and the game begins again. Keep in mind that the challenge rule is not always successful in keeping scores close. Be prepared to rotate players if dominant teams seem to always be forming—but give the challenge rule a chance.

- Play several games simultaneously.

- As an alternative, play a hockey version of World Cup Soccer (page 104).

Think About It

Why the challenge rule? The basis of equalization is that all players have the right to grow. This cannot happen when a team is seriously over- or under-challenged. The purpose is not to end up with a tie every time, but to keep the scores close and make the game more interesting for all players.

Super Scooper

Outdoor

1, 2,   2   1, 2, 3   1   1, 2, 3, 4, 8, 9,
3, 5   11, 15, 20, 24

NASPE 1, 2, 3, 4, 5, 6

Equipment

- 1 milk-jug scooper for each player (tape edges with red or blue tape)
- 2 different-colored Wiffle balls
- 4 cones

Play Space

50 × 100 feet (15 × 30 meters)

Setup

Divide the players into teams of four (two offensive players and two defensive players). Set two cones behind each team to create a goal. Each team has scoopers that are all the same color and a matching ball (using two balls greatly increases the action and spreads the action throughout the field). To make a milk-jug scooper, follow the directions in appendix B (page 145).

How to Play

Similar to Grass Hockey, each team tries to shoot their ball into the opposing goal, and they cannot score in their own goal. Players pass and shoot balls with the scoopers like they would in a game of lacrosse.

The game begins with each team's offensive players facing each other in two lines about 10 feet (3 meters) apart. On the leader's signal, the offensive players without the ball begin to move. The offensive players with their team's ball may not take more than three steps before passing. Defensive players may scoop missed or dropped offensive passes, after which they then take three steps and clear the ball with a long throw. Teams face off after each goal. Each team's offensive and defensive players change positions with every goal scored.

Strategies for Success

- If a team gets two points ahead, the team that is behind institutes a challenge rule. For example, they may decide that the opposing team must double the size of their goal (increasing the winning team's defensive challenge), or that they will decrease the size of their own goal by 50 percent (increasing the winning team's offensive challenge). The losing team can also borrow a player of their choice from the winning team. The challenge rule ends as soon as the deficit is less than two points.

- If a team is four points ahead the game is over. Teams change several players and the game begins again. Keep in mind that the challenge rule is not always successful in keeping scores close. Be prepared to rotate players if dominant teams seem to always be forming—but give the challenge rule a chance.

- Play several games simultaneously.

Ultimate Football

Outdoor

1, 2, 5   **1, 5**   **1, 3, 5, 6**   **1, 3**   **1, 2, 3, 6, 8, 9, 10, 13, 15, 18, 19, 20, 21, 24**

NASPE 1, 2, 3, 4, 5, 6

Equipment

- 1 foam football
- 2 cones
- Pinnies, flags, or socks

Play Space

50 × 100 feet (15 × 30 meters)

Setup

Divide players into two teams of three or four players. Players on one team can wear pinnies, socks, or flags to distinguish them from the other team. Place two cones at the corners of each end of the field to represent the goal lines.

How to Play

The game begins with one team kicking or throwing to the other. The receiving team maintains possession even if they drop the kick or throw. Their task is to move the ball downfield by passing. The player with the ball may not take more than three steps before throwing the ball. No player from the opposing team can guard the thrower (the quarterback). Possession is maintained as long as each pass is complete. The other team takes over possession on an incomplete pass, blocked pass, or interception.

A completed pass into the end zone is a touchdown. When the defensive team takes over possession in the end zone, the other team vacates the end zone. The defensive player taking possession in the end zone may run to the goal line before passing the ball. Players with the ball may run into the end zone as long as they do not take more than three steps.

Strategies for Success

- This game is a variation of Ultimate Frisbee, but the foam footballs are easier for most players to throw and catch.
- Other soft balls may be substituted.
- Allow overhand as well as underhand throws.
- Handoffs are not allowed, as they result in players bunching and colliding.
- Play multiple games simultaneously.

Crossover Volleyball

Indoor

1, 2

1, 4, 5, 8

3, 4, 5, 7, 9

1, 6, 8, 9, 10, 11, 12, 17, 24

NASPE 1, 2, 5, 6

Equipment

- Volleyball poles and nets
- Volleyball trainers or beach balls

Play Space

20 × 40 feet (6 × 12 meters) per game

Setup

Set up the players as in the diagram with 12 players per game, six on each side of the net.

How to Play

Allow player 1 to serve underhand, overhand, or even throw the ball; he can also move a bit closer to the net if necessary. Any misplayed ball results in a point for the other team. If the serving team misplays the ball the other team gets a point and the serve, but teams do not rotate. The teams rotate when player 1 and player 10 have completed service. Player 12 always rotates under the net and becomes the new server at position 1, and player 6 rotates under the net and becomes the new player 7. All 12 players rotate at the same time, as in the diagram.

All players may choose to bump, set, throw, or catch. A catch and throw counts as one hit. Players may also catch, throw to themselves, and then bump or set, which counts as one hit.

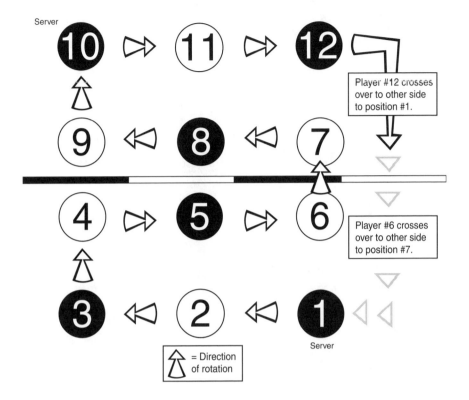

Strategies for Success

- At the conclusion of the game, the scores will likely be close, as most players will have spent part of the game on both the losing and winning sides.

- Many years ago after playing traditional volleyball, a child exited the gym and mumbled (so that I could hear) that she hated volleyball. This version of the game took its full shape the following class. It did not become the young lady's favorite activity, but she no longer dreaded it.

Think About It

How does allowing players to participate at their own level affect willingness to participate, take risks, and attempt a skill at the next higher level? In this game, an opposing player may throw the ball back over the net where in the traditional game the ball would not be returned. How does this affect skill development?

World Cup Soccer

Outdoor

1, 2, 3, 5,   **1, 2, 3, 5**   **1, 2, 3, 9**   **1, 3**   **1, 2, 3, 4, 6,**
   10, 11   **9, 15, 16, 24**

NASPE 1, 2, 3, 4, 5, 6

Equipment

- 2 cones for every team (10 for 5 teams)
- 1 different-colored or marked foam soccer ball for each team
- 4 strips of cloth in the same color for each team (4 red, 4 blue, and so on)

Play Space

Circle with 50-foot (15-meter) radius

Setup

Place one large cone in the center of the circle. Using two cones for each team, place five goals in a circle around the center cone. Goals should be about 8 feet (2.5 meters) wide. Divide the group into five teams of four or five players. Each team has two defenders and two forwards. One defensive player is allowed to be the goalie and use the hands. A team of five players would have two defenders, two forwards, and one goalie. Each team is given a goal to defend. Place the four strips of cloth on the top of each team's goal cones.

How to Play

The game begins with the offensive players from each team dribbling their ball out to score on each of the other four teams. Offensive players start play from in front of their goal. Defensive players may kick balls away from the goal they are defending, but offensive players may never kick another team's ball. If the ball goes higher than the goalie's shoulders, no point is scored. When a goal is scored, the offensive team takes one of the cloth strips and proceeds to another goal, following no particular order. Goalies may pick up a ball and punt or throw it. When a team has collected one cloth strip from

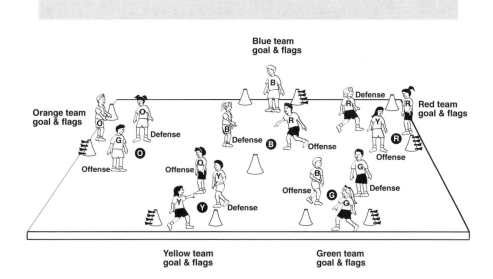

Blue team
goal & flags

Orange team
goal & flags

Red team
goal & flags

Defense

Defense

Offense

Defense

Defense

Offense

Offense

Offense

Defense

Defense

Yellow team
goal & flags

Green team
goal & flags

each of the opposing teams, they run to the middle and hold up the strips, signaling that they have won.

Strategies for Success

- In the second round, have all offensive and defensive players switch roles.

- For round 3, rotate a few players from each team to the next.

- If a team loses all their cloth strips but the game is not over, their defense may go out to assist their offense.

- I only use foam soccer balls. With this much action, foam soccer balls significantly reduce injuries and eliminate any emotional fear.

Think About It

In traditional soccer games there is one ball and 10, 11, or 12 players per side. When a player makes a mistake, everyone sees it. This can cause a player to withdraw from the activity, or worse, from physical activity in general. In this version there is so much action that players are not watching just a few players. Players can make mistakes without the embarrassment, which encourages perseverance and risk taking.

Group Initiatives

Group initiatives have been around for a long time but have become especially popular in the last 10 years. Many initiatives allow participants to choose whether they wish to accept the challenge. Those who choose not to accept don't get much from the activity. However, a teacher can encourage students to take the challenge by offering alternatives and different levels of challenge that meet the needs of all students. This chapter's initiatives contain inclusive modifications that address children's social, emotional, cognitive, and physical needs.

Present the initiatives as part of a circuit. You can set up four different initiatives around the playing area or one initiative for every six players. Divide the players into four teams of six and give them a certain amount of time to work on an initiative. When time is up, the players return the equipment to its starting position and rotate to the next station. Groups will have another opportunity during the following class to try the same initiative, possibly at a different level of challenge.

You need to make sure the rules are strictly followed if you want to meet the activity's objectives. It is often necessary to restate the rules. Laminating the rules on poster board is quite helpful.

Finally, you should never coach solutions to initiatives.

Ahhh Bucket!

Indoor or outdoor

1, 2, 4, 7,   **1, 5**   **2, 3, 4,**   **2**
9, 11, 13   **5, 7**

NASPE 2, 3, 4, 5, 6

Equipment

- 5-gallon (19-liter) paint bucket
- 1 piece of rope, 30 feet (9 meters) long
- 5-pound (2.25-kilogram) weight
- Floor tape (inside) or field paint (outside)

Play Space

20 × 40 feet (6 × 12 meters)

Setup

Using floor tape (inside) or field paint (outside), mark a circle with a 15-foot (5-meter) diameter. Place the bucket in the center of the circle. Lay the rope on the ground on the outside of the circle. Put the weight in the bucket to keep it from tipping over or sliding.

How to Play

All players spread out along the rope and grab the rope with both hands. Players may not enter the circle, but they may slide their hands up and down the rope as long as they do not let go of the rope or trade places. The group must figure out how to remove the bucket by lifting it out of the circle. The bucket may not be thrown or dragged.

Strategies for Success

- If the bucket slides more than 2 feet (0.6 meters), move it back to the center.
- Placing a poly spot under the bucket also helps prevent sliding.
- Players are often tempted to release the rope and put a hand somewhere other than where it is supposed to be. Be watchful.

Big Wheel

Indoor or outdoor

1, 2, 4, 5,
8, 9, 10, 11

1, 5

2, 3, 4,
5, 7

2

NASPE 2, 3, 4, 5, 6

Equipment
2 segmented tumbling mats that Velcro to each other

Play Space
12 × 60 feet (4 × 18 meters)

Setup
Place the mats, unattached and folded, on the floor behind the starting line. Use two mats per team if doing the activity with more than one team. Teams should have five to eight players.

How to Play
The team must construct a vehicle that will transport them across the room so that only the tumbling mats touch the floor. For example, the team might lay one mat out upside down, place the other mat on top, Velcro the ends together, get inside, lift the top with their hands, and walk as the mat rotates like the wheel of an army tank.

Strategies for Success
- Don't be surprised if the players come up with a totally different solution than the one described in How to Play.
- Do not coach the answer. A picture can stimulate thinking, so I use a picture of an army tank, though I don't say, "Build one of these."

- If players touch the ground, the team can choose to go back to the start or proceed. If they decide to proceed, the team is assessed a penalty point. If they get across the gym with five penalty points, the next time they try the activity they are challenged to get across with less than five penalty points.
- The width of a basketball court has proven to be an effective distance to cross.

Cliffhanger

Indoor

4, 5, 7, 11

1, 3, 8

2, 3

2, 3

NASPE 2, 3, 4, 5, 6

Equipment

- 4 or more horizontal rock-climbing panels, 4 × 8 feet (1 × 2.5 meters)
- Tumbling mats (enough to cover the area under the wall)

Play Space

Wall and floor space to allow 6 feet (1.8 meters) of mats on the floor and at least 4 rock-climbing panels on the wall

Setup

Place the mats on the floor along the entire length of the wall. The floor *must* be padded. Draw a horizontal line 3 to 4 feet (1 to 1.2 meters) up the wall and do not allow players to put their feet above this line.

This activity works best as one station of four so that there are 5, 6, or 7 participants at the wall. Quite often there will be 3 or 4 climbers on the wall at the same time.

How to Play

My school is fortunate enough to have six of these panels, making the total rock traverse 24 feet (7 meters). Color-coded rocks make planning courses much easier. Players traverse the wall one at a time. The next player may not begin until the player ahead gets to the third panel. No passing is allowed. Players who fall off must go to the end of the line and restart.

Level 1—Use any and all colors of rocks. Hand- and footholds should be close enough and large enough so that with a modest amount of effort everyone can have some degree of success.

Level 2—Eliminate the use of all rocks of a certain color.

Level 3—Eliminate the use of all rocks of two colors. Provide fewer large holds for the feet, causing the upper body to work harder, and spread holds farther apart.

Level 4 and beyond—Use only certain rocks; get creative!

Strategies for Success

Climbing walls are rather expensive, but they could be made by your district's carpenters using sanded and coated plywood and purchased hand- and foot-holds.

Carry On

Indoor or outdoor

1, 2, 4, 5,   **1, 5, 6**   **2, 3, 4,**   **2, 3**
9, 10, 11   **5, 7**

NASPE 2, 3, 4, 5, 6

Equipment

None

Play Space

10 × 60 feet (3 × 18 meters)

Setup

Draw two parallel lines at opposite ends of the playing area (the width of a basketball court works well). Divide the group into teams of 6, 7, or 8 players and place them behind the starting line at one end of the playing area.

How to Play

This is a "get from here to there" type of problem. To get to the other side of the playing area, a player must be carried. All carriers must return to the start, and eventually they must also be carried. The problem is how to get the entire team to the other side. When only one carrier remains, that player may walk to the other side without being carried.

   No player is allowed on another player's shoulders. No running is allowed.

Strategies for Success

- Briefly discuss the biomechanics of lifting with the legs as opposed to the back and why it's better to lift with the legs.
- Each trip to the other side counts as a point. The goal is to complete the problem with as few points possible. Each team is challenged to better their previous record.
- If a player who is being carried touches the floor, he and the carriers must return to the start, though they are not penalized with a point.

- Do not coach the answer. I usually give the following example and simply say that there is *something* that the players could do to make one trip instead of two: If Charlie and Marjorie are carrying Rose and at the same time Luke and Matthew are carrying Raelyn, this would count as two trips. However, if Charlie, Marjorie, or Rose held hands or in some other way connected with Luke, Matthew, and Raelyn, it would only count as one trip.

- Be very sensitive to weight issues. Make sure that you do not place a larger player in a group of much smaller players.

Mushroom River

Indoor or outdoor

1, 2, 4, 5, 8, **1, 5, 6** **2, 3, 4,** **15**
9, 10, 11, 13 **5, 7, 9**

NASPE 1, 2, 5, 6

Equipment

1 carpet square or poly spot per player (6 or more)

Play Space

10 × 40 feet (3 × 12 meters)

Setup

Divide the group into teams of six. Each player receives a carpet square, or magic mushroom. Use cones or floor tape to designate a starting line and finish line, 20 to 30 feet (6 to 9 meters) apart.

How to Play

Teams must get to the finish line without any body part touching the ground unprotected. The magic mushrooms may touch the ground, and they protect any body part touching it. However, the magic mushrooms only maintain their magical protective powers as long as they have human contact. If a player has part of one foot on the magic mushroom and part on the ground, that foot is still protected. Likewise, if a thumb is on the magic mushroom and the other fingers of the same hand are touching the floor, that hand is protected. However, if the right foot is protected and the left foot touches the floor without any part of the left foot in contact with the magic mushroom, the player is sent back because the left foot touched the ground and was not protected.

If at any time the mushroom completely loses human contact, even for a split second, the team loses that mushroom. The player who lost the mushroom must return to the start and cross as a part of the team.

Players may not slide or hop with the carpet squares, and they cannot use their shoelaces to tie the carpet square to their feet.

Strategies for Success

- Resist the temptation to coach answers to the problem. Carefully directed questions can focus the group.
- Strict adherence to the rules enhances critical-thinking skills.
- If a team successfully completes the task, begin the next round with one less magic mushroom.
- For groups that are ready, challenge the players to get to the other side and then return.

Nuclear Waste Disposal

Indoor or outdoor

**1, 2, 4, 5,
8, 9, 10, 11**

1, 5

**2, 3, 4,
5, 7, 9**

2

NASPE 2, 3, 4, 5, 6

Equipment

- 4-foot (1.2-meter) square piece of plywood with a hole in the center and 3-foot (1 meter) ropes attached to each side (see page 146 in appendix B)
- 1 foam die
- 1 football
- 1 tennis ball
- 2 cones

Play Space

12 × 60 feet (4 × 18 meters)

Setup

Use the cones to designate starting and finish lines (the width of a basketball court works well). Place the square behind the starting line with the ropes stretched out on each side. Tie a knot in each rope 3 feet (1 meter) from the point where the rope ties into the wood. Players may not grab the rope closer to the wood than this knot. Up to 8 players stand around the wood. Place the die, or nuclear waste, on the wood.

How to Play

In this activity the group must transport the nuclear waste across the playing area. Players spread out around the wood and grab the ropes. Players may hold more than one rope, but they may not hold ropes from different sides of the wood. Players may not contact the wood with any part of their body. Players must lift the transport and carry the nuclear waste without spilling or touching it.

Strategies for Success

- If the object falls off the transport the group scores a negative point.
- In subsequent attempts players try to improve on the previous score.
- When they master the die, the group should move on to the football, and then the tennis ball.
- If groups successfully transport the tennis ball, try putting two or three golf balls on at the same time.

Half-Pipe

Indoor or outdoor

1, 2, 4, 9,   **5, 6**   **2, 4, 5, 9**   **2**
11, 12, 13

NASPE 2, 3, 4, 5, 6

Equipment

- 1 section of hollow carpet tube, newspaper core, or PVC pipe for each player, cut in half lengthwise (see page 146 in appendix B)
- Several small rubber balls, table-tennis balls, tennis balls
- 2 5-gallon (19-liter) buckets for each team

Play Space

10 × 60 feet (3 × 18 meters)

Setup

Form teams of 5, 6, or 7 players. The team's objective is to transport as many balls across the playing area as possible in the allotted amount of time. Place a bucket of balls at the starting line and an empty bucket 50 feet (15 meters) away, at the finish line.

How to Play

Give each player a half pipe. The first player holds his pipe and is the only player who can pick up a ball. He places the ball in his pipe and then holds the pipe so that the ball travels from one end to the other. The second player should be in position to receive the ball with her pipe without touching the ball with her hands. The ball is passed from one player's pipe to the next until the last player tips his pipe so that the ball lands in the bucket. The player with the ball in his pipe cannot travel with it (walk, run, and so on). A dropped ball must be restarted from the beginning.

Strategies for Success

- No players should be skipped at any time. All players should have a turn passing the ball with each passing order. With five players the passing order would be 1-2-3-4-5-1-2-3-4-5-1-2-3-4-5. Players should not stop passing to watch, creating a passing order that looks something like 1-2-3-4-5-1-2-3-1-2-3-1-2-1-2.

- Try using full pipes. Not seeing the ball makes the challenge much more difficult.

Roller Coaster

Indoor

1, 2, 4, 5, 8,
9, 10, 11

1, 5

2, 3, 4,
5, 7

2

NASPE 2, 3, 4, 5, 6

Equipment

- 6 to 8 heavy-duty newspaper cores, 4 to 5 inches (10 to 13 centimeters) in diameter; ask for these at your local newspaper
- 1 piece of wood, 2 inches × 12 inches × 10 feet (5 centimeters × 30.5 centimeters × 3 meters)
- 25 to 30 feet (8 to 9 meters) of rope
- 10-foot (3-meter) PVC pipe, 2 inches (5 centimeters) in diameter
- Tape or cones

Play Space

10 × 40 feet (3 × 12 meters)

Setup

Divide the group into teams of 5, 6, or 7. Place all equipment at one end of the playing area. Designate starting and finish lines with tape or cones. Tie one end of the rope to a heavy, stationary object, such as bleachers or a game standard, just beyond the finish line. Place the other end of the rope at the starting line.

How to Play

Teams must use the roller coaster (wood) to transport the group from one side of the amusement park (play space) to the other, or about 25 to 30 feet (8 to 9 meters). No player may touch the ground. If a player falls off the roller coaster (touches the ground), she must return to the start. All equipment except the roller coaster is allowed to touch the ground. If the roller coaster is derailed (touches the ground), all players must return to the start and begin again.

Strategies for Success

- Do not allow players to stand on equipment, especially the wood and the newspaper cores. Players can sit, kneel, lie down, squat, and so on, but not stand. This will help keep the players from falling.
- Groups do not have to use all the equipment.
- I have had many players try kneeling on the newspaper cores and sliding across the floor. Watch them carefully, as their toes almost always touch the ground sooner or later.
- Teams must retrieve any player who has fallen off and returned to the start.

Honey, I Shrunk the Landing

Indoor

1, 2, 4, 5,   **1, 5**   **2, 4, 5, 7**   **2**   **15**
9, 10, 11

NASPE 1, 2, 3, 4, 5, 6

Equipment

- 1 swinging rope, properly designed and installed for swinging
- 2 folding gymnastics mats, 5 × 12 feet (1.5 × 3.5 meters)
- 2 folding gymnastics mats, 4 × 8 feet (1 × 2.5 meters)
- An old vaulting buck or pommel horse with pommels removed (see appendix B, page 147)

Play Space

10 × 25 feet (3 × 8 meters)

Setup

Divide players into groups of 5, 6, 7, or 8. Place the vaulting buck at the far reach of the swinging rope (far enough that players standing on the buck can grasp the rope and swing with their feet on the rope's bottom while not striking their bottom on the buck). With the large mats, cover the floor directly below the area where the players will swing. Place one of the smaller mats on top of the far end of the other mats. Place the second smaller mat on the approach side of the vaulting buck (where the players wait).

How to Play

In this activity, the members of a group swing one at a time on the rope and land on the designated mat. When a player swings to the landing mat, he must stay on the mat without stepping off and touching the gym floor or the large protective mats. If a player steps off or in any way falls off the landing mat, the entire group must return to the start. When all players have landed on the mat, the group counts to five and the problem is solved.

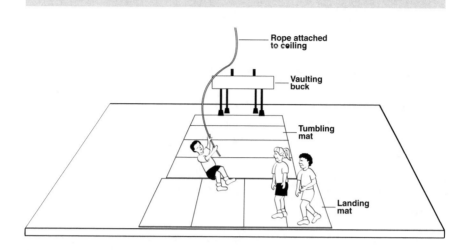

Rope attached to ceiling

Vaulting buck

Tumbling mat

Landing mat

Strategies for Success

- If the group solves the problem, fold one section of the landing mat. When they solve that problem, fold another section. This gradually increases the difficulty of the challenge whenever the group is ready. As the landing mat shrinks, players discover how much support and help they need from each other to keep the group from falling off the mat.

- For safety, allow only one swing on the rope before landing.

- Place a soft landing mat on the approach side of the vaulting buck in case a student falls backward off the vault.

- If a player swings to the landing mat and knocks another player off, the group must return to the start. I often ask the group if there was anything they could have done to keep the player from falling off. This often stimulates teamwork strategies.

- Some players are intimidated by rope swinging, so you should have an alternative route to the landing mat. Tie a rope to a game standard located just beyond the landing zone and have players sit on a carpet square to pull themselves hand over hand to the landing mat. Or, you could place poly spots or stepping stones on the gym floor and have players hop from one spot to another to get to the landing mat.

Based on Karl Rohnke, 1989. *Cowtails and Cobras II: A Guide to Games, Initiatives, Rope Courses, and Adventure Curriculum* (Dubuque, IA: Kendall/Hunt).

Jungle Swing

Indoor

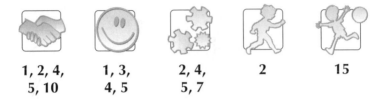

| 1, 2, 4, 5, 10 | 1, 3, 4, 5 | 2, 4, 5, 7 | 2 | 15 |

NASPE 2, 3, 4, 5, 6

Equipment

- 2 swinging ropes, properly designed and installed for swinging
- 4 gymnastics mats, 5 × 12 feet (1.5 × 3.5 meters)
- An old vaulting buck or other stable platform (see appendix B, page 147)

Play Space

10 × 30 feet (3 × 9 meters)

Setup

Divide players into groups of 5, 6, 7, or 8. Place the vaulting buck at one end of the arc made by the swinging rope. Players should be able to stand on top of the vault and comfortably grasp the rope while placing the rope between their legs. If the vault is too close to the rope, the players will strike their backside on the vault as they swing.

Place two mats end to end to cover the swinging path of the rope. Fold the third mat (the landing mat) and place it on top of the second mat, near the end. Place a mat on the approach side of the vault.

How to Play

Players must swing from the first rope to the second and then land on the folded mat. When the entire team has landed on the folded mat, they have solved the challenge. If a player falls off the rope onto the tumbling mats, not the folded landing mat, the entire team must start over. If the players successfully solve the problem, move the folded mat a bit farther away.

Strategies for Success

Providing an alternative to swinging on the rope for those players who do not want to swing is both socially and emotionally important. You could use poly spots, stepping stones, or a low balance beam, placing these items to the side of the protective mats and out of the swinging path. Players can hop from poly spot to poly spot, traverse the balance beam, or jump from stepping stone to stepping stone to get to the landing mat. I do not allow any player using the alternative to be the last one across so that they can be on the landing mat to assist other teammates and be a contributing member of the team.

Adapted, by permission, from D. Glover and D. Midura, 1992, *Team building through physical challenges* (Champaign, IL: Human Kinetics), 65.

Missing Bridge

Indoor or outdoor

1, 2, 4, 5,   1, 3, 4, 5   2, 3, 4,   2   15
8, 9, 10, 11   5, 7

NASPE 1, 2, 5, 6

Equipment

- 4 car tires
- 3 pieces of wood, 2 inches × 6 inches × 8 feet (5 centimeters × 15 centimeters × 2.5 meters)
- Cones or floor tape

Play Space

10 × 40 feet (3 × 12 meters)

Setup

Use cones or floor tape to designate starting and finish lines, 20 to 30 feet (6 to 9 meters) apart. Space the tires equally across the space between the starting and finish lines. The first tire should be about 3 feet (1 meter) from the starting line and the last tire should be 3 feet (1 meter) away from the finish line. Place a group of 5, 6, 7, or 8 players at the starting line with the pieces of wood.

How to Play

Using the pieces of wood, the group must cross the distance without touching the floor or moving the tires. Players may stand on the tires. The problem is not solved until all players reach the finish. A player who touches the floor must return to the start and is not allowed to bring a piece of wood with him.

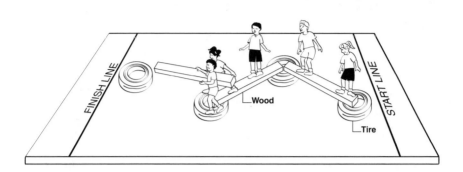

Strategies for Success

- Players are not allowed to jump on or off a tire.
- Players cannot stand or walk on the wood if the wood is touching the ground between the start and finish lines.
- If a team successfully solves the problem, have them make another attempt with one less piece of wood. It is possible to solve the problem with only one piece of wood, but it will take some excellent planning and teamwork.

The Wall

Indoor

1, 2, 4,
9, 10, 11

1, 3, 4,
5, 7, 8

2, 3, 4,
5, 7, 9

2, 3

NASPE 2, 3, 4, 5, 6

Equipment

- An old set of parallel bars
- 9 gymnastics mats, 5 × 12 feet (1.5 × 3.5 meters)
- 1 landing mat, 5 feet × 10 feet × 12 inches thick (1.5 meters × 3 meters × 30 centimeters thick)
- Duct tape

Play Space

12 × 14 feet (3.5 × 4 meters)

Setup

Form groups of 5, 6, 7, or 8 players. Raise the parallel bars as high as possible and turn bars inward so they are close together. Lay two folded mats on top, end to end, and then put one more on the top of one of them. About 18 inches (46 centimeters) from the end of each mat, wrap duct tape over the top of the mats and under the parallel bars. Go around 5 to 10 times until the mats are securely in place. Drape two more mats over the top so that they hang down on either side. Place a crash mat on one side of "the wall" and stack two open tumbling mats on the other side. Open the final tumbling mat and place it perpendicular to the other mats so that it goes under the wall and sticks out on both sides.

How to Play

The group must get all players over the wall. No player may stand on the wall or stay on top of it. To get off the top, a player turns around, sits, and jumps onto the crash mat. Players who have gotten to the other side must come back, but they are not allowed to lift anyone over. Instead they are to spot players who have not yet gone over. As more and more players make it over the wall,

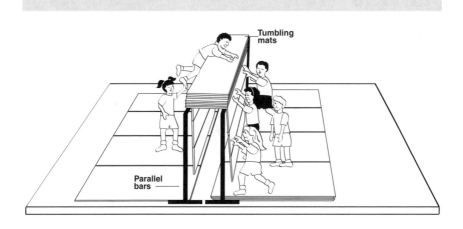

fewer and fewer are left to help lift a player. The last player may select one of the players who already went over to help. If the players are successful, they should try again, but go in a different order. Or, ask if anyone who went over the smaller section wants to try going over the taller section. For those not wanting to go over the wall, have an alternate route for getting to the other side, such as a small balance beam to the side or some stepping stones (see Turtleback River, page 138). No one may use the alternative until they have helped all who want to go over the wall.

Strategies for Success

The rule about not using the alternative route until players have helped others go over the wall keeps these players from devaluing themselves. Simply walking across to the other side means they have not been of help to their team. I have seen many players not climb the wall but still serve as valuable and desired team members.

Tire Transport

Indoor or outdoor

1, 2, 4, 5, 7,   **1, 4, 5, 8**   **2, 3, 4, 5, 7**   **15**
9, 10, 11, 13

NASPE 1, 2, 5, 6

Equipment

- 1 car tire for each participant
- Floor tape or cones

Play Space

10 × 40 feet (3 × 12 meters)

Setup

Mark off an area about 30 feet (9 meters) long and 10 feet (3 meters) wide, using cones or floor tape to designate starting and finish lines. Place the tires behind the starting line. Play with groups of 5, 6, 7, or 8.

How to Play

The group must cross the distance without touching the floor. Players who touch the floor must return to the beginning, and they are not allowed to bring a tire back. More than one player may be on a tire at a time. Players may not stand on the floor in the tire center, because placing the foot inside the tire rim can cause injury.

Strategies for Success

- When a player returns to the start, the remaining team members must problem solve to rescue that player. Do not coach an answer. A simple reminder that the group cannot solve the problem unless everyone gets to the other side is often enough to get the thinking process started.

- Groups of six or seven players have made it across using only two tires, a level appropriate for their ability.

- I have had players at the finish line ask if they are allowed to go back and help some of the stranded players. Of course I say yes. These thoughtful players then pick up a tire and begin to walk across the floor to go back and help. When I remind them they cannot touch the floor, I can really see the wheels begin to turn inside their head.

- If a team successfully solves the problem, have them repeat it with one less tire each subsequent effort.

Adapted, by permission, from D. Glover and D. Midura, 1992, *Team building through physical challenges* (Champaign, IL: Human Kinetics), 43.

All Mixed Up

Indoor or outdoor

1, 2, 3, 4, 8,   1, 3, 5   2, 3, 4,   15
9, 10, 11, 13   5, 7

NASPE 1, 2, 5, 6

Equipment

- 1 small and 1 large balance beam or suitable substitutes
- Several tumbling mats
- Tape
- A 2-inch × 6-inch × 10-foot (5-centimeter × 15-centimeter × 3-meter) board (place flat on the ground if playing outside)

Play Space

12 × 12 feet (4 × 4 meters)

Setup

Tape a 4-inch × 8-foot (10-centimeter × 2.5-meter) line on the floor. Place the balance beams close by and put mats under the balance beams. Play with a team of 6, 7, or 8 players.

How to Play

Before beginning the group must decide to do either the floor tape or balance beam. Teams may change their minds based on team success or failure. The players stand side by side on the balance beam or the line on the floor, whichever they choose. The challenge is for player 1 to exchange positions with player 6, the last person. Player 2 trades with player 5 and 3 trades with 4. If you have an odd number of players, the center player stays in position while the others pass. All this must be accomplished without any player falling off the beam or stepping off the line on the floor. The taller beam is a greater challenge and leads to even greater creativity.

Strategies for Success

- When players fall they must return to where they started. Or, simply allow them to get back on and have the group count the number of falls. They can then try to do better on a subsequent trial.
- Don't tell the players what the challenge is until they are on the beam.
- After the team mounts the beam, try arranging by different challenges:
  - Alphabetical order
  - Height
  - Birth date

Think About It

Traditionally you might have fourth graders use the line on the floor, fifth graders use the low beam, and sixth graders use the high beam. However, this is most likely developmentally inappropriate for some children in all three grades, so let the players select their level of challenge.

Trolleys

Indoor or outdoor

1, 2, 4, 5,   **1, 5**   **2, 4, 5, 7**   **2**   **15**
9, 10, 11

NASPE 1, 2, 3, 4, 5, 6

Equipment

- Large trolley
- Small trolley

Note: Trolleys are commercially available but not nearly as strong as the homemade versions (see p. 145 in appendix B).

Play Space

10 × 40 feet (3 × 12 meters)

Setup

Divide the group into teams of six. Designate starting and finish lines about 30 feet (9 meters) apart. Place the trolleys on the ground at the starting line. The large trolley can accommodate six players and the smaller can accommodate three players. Place the two pieces of wood parallel to each other.

How to Play

Players stand with their right foot on one piece and their left on another. Each player grasps the right and left ropes in front of them. The team must then walk in unison across a given distance. If a player falls off the wood, a point is counted against the team.

Strategies for Success

- A group of six players will usually find it easier to place three players on each set of small trolleys than all 6 on the large. However, it should be the group's choice.
- Each team counts their own points, if they want.
- Challenge the group to go the distance backward, sideways, or in any combination.

Turtleback River

Indoor or outdoor

1, 2, 4, 5   **1, 3, 5**   **2, 3, 4,**   **15**
                                        5, 7

NASPE 1, 2, 5, 6

Equipment

- 2 tumbling mats, 6 × 12 feet (1.8 × 3.5 meters) or grass field
- 3 hard shell domes (the turtles) for each player

Note: Picture a ball cut in half, but made of hard plastic; these are usually available under various names through physical education equipment companies.

Play Space

10 × 40 feet (3 × 12 meters)

Setup

Divide players into groups of 5, 6, 7, or 8. If playing outside, mark an area about 24 feet (7 meters) long and 6 feet (1.8 meters) wide. If playing inside, place the tumbling mats end to end. Each player begins with three turtles each.

How to Play

The group's objective is to cross the raging river (the floor) without falling in. Players may step only on the hard shell of the turtle's back. If a player falls into the river, she must return to the start and remove the turtle closest to the start. This turtle may not be used again. The group does not solve the problem until all players are across the river. Players are allowed to share turtles; however, you should not tell the group that. Instead, let the group come to that solution on their own.

Strategies for Success

- The plastic domes are slippery on a gym floor, and the tumbling mats prevent sliding.
- Every time a group solves the problem they begin again but increase the challenge:
  - All players start with two turtles each
  - All players start with one turtle each
  - All players start with one turtle except one player, who has none

Appendix A

Development Objectives and NASPE Standards

In each game, you'll find a list of numbers underneath the icons. Find the corresponding numbers in the following lists to verify the objectives of the game. The recently revised NASPE standards are listed in their entirety after the objectives.

Socialization Skills

Socialization = NASPE 5 and 6

1. Working as part of a team
2. Working toward a common goal
3. Sharing space
4. Listening to others
5. Self-refereeing
6. Setting up rules
7. Abiding by the rules
8. Compromising
9. Expressing oneself
10. Helping others or being helped by others
11. Offering suggestions
12. Cooperating
13. Collaborating

Emotional Development

Emotional development = NASPE 5 and 6

1. Participating at one's own level of ability
2. Focusing off failure
3. Feeling physically safe
4. Feeling socially safe
5. Having a sense of belonging
6. Laughing at self and group—easily forgiving mistakes
7. Trusting
8. Taking a risk

Cognitive Skills

Cognitive = NASPE 2

1. Motor planning
2. Developing strategies
3. Decision making
4. Analyzing and evaluating
5. Generating alternatives
6. Anticipating and predicting
7. Problem solving
8. Reinforcing classroom lessons (math, spelling, social studies, and so on)
9. Attending and concentrating

Physical Fitness

Physical = NASPE 1, 2, 3, 4

1. Performing enjoyable, large muscle mass, intermittent, moderate to vigorous physical activity
2. Exercising the upper body
3. Exercising the lower body
4. Building abdominal strength and endurance
5. Increasing range of motion

Sport Skill Practice

Sport skill = NASPE 1

1. Eye–hand–object coordination
2. Motor planning
3. Agility
4. Body and space relationships
5. Auditory acuity
6. Temporal (timing) awareness
7. Pattern recognition
8. Reading the parabolic path
9. Visual tracking
10. Force development
11. Angle of projection
12. Knowledge of contact points
13. Follow-through
14. Flattening the swinging arc
15. Static and dynamic balance

16. Visual figure or ground discrimination
17. Rebound angles
18. Throwing
19. Catching
20. Opposition
21. Force absorption
22. Spatial awareness
23. Auditory figure or ground discrimination
24. Object manipulation

National Standards for Physical Education

Physical activity is critical to the development and maintenance of good health. The goal of physical education is to develop physically educated individuals who have the knowledge, skills, and confidence to enjoy a lifetime of healthful physical activity. A physically educated person meets the following standards:

Standard 1
Demonstrates competency in motor skills and movement patterns needed to perform a variety of physical activities.

Standard 2
Demonstrates understanding of movement concepts, principles, strategies, and tactics as they apply to the learning and performance of physical activities.

Standard 3
Participates regularly in physical activity.

Standard 4
Achieves and maintains a health-enhancing level of physical fitness.

Standard 5
Exhibits responsible personal and social behavior that respects self and others in physical activity settings.

Standard 6
Values physical activity for health, enjoyment, challenge, self-expression, and/or social interaction.

Reprinted from *Moving Into the Future: National Standards for Physical Education*, 2nd Edition (2004) with permission from the National Association for Sport and Physical Education (NASPE), 1900 Association Drive, Reston, VA 20191-1599.

Appendix B

Equipment List

Homemade Equipment

The following equipment will need to be made ahead of time to play some of the games in this book.

1. Panty-Hose Tennis Rackets

For each racket you will need a sturdy wire coat hanger, an old pair of washed panty hose, and duct tape. Bend the hook of the hanger to close the loop. Hold the hanger with your index finger where the hook meets the body of the hanger. With your other index finger, grab the middle of the wire where you would hang a pair of pants. Pull at these two points to stretch the coat hanger. Cut the tops off the panty hose so that you are using just the legs. Stretch a leg over the hanger and wrap the excess around the neck of the hook. Grab the corners of the hanger (where the shoulders of a shirt would hang) and pull to form a diamond shape. Use duct tape to keep the hose from unraveling at the neck. Several panty hose manufacturers have been known to donate defective hose (legs only) to schools and community organizations.

2. Carpet Squares

See your local carpet store for old samples that can be cut into squares. Using a utility knife, cut the carpets into squares approximately 6 × 12 inches (15 × 30 centimeters).

3. Milk-Jug Scoopers

Completely wash 1-gallon (3.8-liter) plastic milk jugs with soap and water. Using scissors cut the bottom 1 to 2 inches (2 to 5 centimeters) off each container. Cover the cut edge with duct tape to prevent injuries.

4. Trolleys

Trolleys are commercially available from any physical education catalog; however they are expensive and not very strong. Two 2-inch × 6-inch × 8-foot (5-centimeter × 15-centimeter × 2.5-meter) pieces of wood will make a trolley that holds six students. Drill a 0.5-inch (1.27-centimeter) hole through the center of the wood 2 inches (5 centimeters) from one end. Drill five more holes every 15 inches (38 centimeters). On the bottom of each piece of wood use a 1-inch (2-centimeter) wood boring bit to countersink each hole.

Take a 48-inch (1.2-meter) piece of 3/8-inch (1-centimeter) poly rope and slide it through the first hole. On the underside (the side with the countersunk hole), tie several knots so that the rope cannot be pulled back through the hole but still fits inside the hole so that the wood will lie flat on the floor. Tie a knot on the top side of the wood so that the rope does not go through the hole in either direction. Tie a knot at the upper end of each rope. Repeat for each hole.

Two 2-inch × 6-inch × 4-foot (5-centimeter × 15-centimeter × 1.2-meter) pieces of wood will make a trolley that holds three students. The process is the same as for the larger trolley.

5. Pipeline
You will need a 3-foot (1-meter) piece of PVC pipe with a 4- to 6-inch (10- to 15-centimeter) diameter for each player. Using a jigsaw, cut each piece of pipe in half vertically so that you end up with two 3-foot (1-meter) half-pipes. Tape the edges with duct tape or sand them smooth to prevent injuries.

6. Nuclear Waste Disposal
On a 4- × 4-foot (1.2- × 1.2-meter) piece of 3/8-inch (1-centimeter) plywood, mark the center and inscribe a circle with a 1-foot (30.5-centimeter) diameter. Drill a hole through the center of the circle. Fit your jigsaw through that hole and cut out the 1-foot (30.5-centimeter) center hole. Two inches (5 centimeters) from the edge and 6 inches (15 centimeters) from the corner, drill a .5-inch (1.25-centimeter) hole. Drill three more holes down the same side every 12 inches (30.5 centimeters) for a total of four holes. Repeat on each side. Use duct tape to tape the rough edges of the wood or sand them smooth to prevent splinters. Loop and tie a 3-foot (1-meter) rope through each hole. Tie knots in the end of each rope to prevent unraveling.

Unusual Items

Several games in this book use some unusual items that the reader is advised to collect ahead of time:

Automobile tires

Bath towels

Boxes

Deck tennis rings (available through most physical education equipment companies—they look like large rubber doughnuts)

Dom Ringette stick

Foam pipe insulation (available at hardware stores)

Hard shell domes

Newspaper cores (ask your local newspaper to donate them)

Paint bucket, 5-gallon (19-liter) (sold at hardware stores as storage containers)

Parallel bars (check with your local high school gymnastics coach or any of the local gymnastics schools for old equipment)

PVC pipe, 10 inches (25 centimeters) long, 2 inches (5 centimeters) in diameter

Refrigerator-sized cardboard boxes (remove any protruding staples)

Rubber chickens

Soda bottles, 1- and 2-liter

Soda bottle caps or milk caps, plastic

Stuffed toy animal of a coyote

Tube socks

Vaulting buck (check with your local high school gymnastics coach or any of the local gymnastics schools for old equipment)

Water-balloon slingshots

Wood, 2 inches × 12 inches × 10 feet (5 centimeters × 30.5 centimeters × 3 meters)

Wood, 2 inches × 6 inches × 8 feet (5 centimeters × 15 centimeters × 2.5 meters)

Appendix C

Assessment Tools

Assessment of Enjoyment Report

Table C.1 Enjoyment

Game	Average enjoyment score	Number of students
Hoop Tag	4.23	122
Foot Fencing	3.93	118
Dee Fence	3.68	125
Where'd They Go?	3.96	121
Capture the Flag	4.46	342
Around the World Basketball	4.25	66

Grade the Grame

Girl _____   Room number _____

Boy _____   Heart monitor # _____

Please circle the face that best answers each of the following questions:

1. How did you like the game?

Terrible   No good   Just OK   Good   Great

2. How would you feel about playing this game again in class?

Terrible   No good   Just OK   Good   Great

3. Would you play this game when not in school (with friends, parents, or at a picnic)?

Terrible   No good   Just OK   Good   Great

From *Games for the Whole Child*, by Dr. Brian Barrett, 2005, Champaign, IL: Human Kinetics.

References

Bar-Or, O. 1983. *Pediatric sports medicine for the practitioner: From physiologic principles to clinical applications.* New York: Springer-Verlag.

Blair, S.N., D.G. Clark, K.J. Cureton, and K.E. Powell. 1989. Exercise and fitness in childhood: Implications for a lifetime of health. In *Perspectives in exercise science and sports medicine: Vol. 2. Youth, exercise, and sport,* eds. C.V. Gisolfi and D.R. Lamb. Indianapolis: Benchmark Press.

Caine, R.N., and G. Caine. 2003. Principles wheel: The brain/mind learning principles. http://cainelearning.com/pwheel (accessed August 6, 2004).

Council of Physical Education for Children (COPEC). 1992. *Developmentally appropriate physical education practices for children.* Reston, VA: NASPE.

Council of Physical Education for Children (COPEC). 1998. *Physical activity for children: A statement of guidelines.* National Association for Sport and Physical Education. Reston, VA.

Goleman, D. 1995. *Emotional intelligence: Why it can matter more than IQ.* New York: Bantam Books.

Hellison, D. 2003. *Teaching responsibility through physical activity.* 2nd ed. Champaign, IL: Human Kinetics.

National Association for Sport and Physical Education (NASPE). 1998. *Physical activity for children: A statement of guidelines.* Reston, VA: NASPE.

National Association for the Education of Young Children (NAEYC). 1987. *Developmentally appropriate practice in early childhood programs serving children from birth through age 8: Expanded edition.* Washington, DC: NAEYC.

Pate, R.R., and R.C. Hohn. 1994. *Health and fitness through physical education.* Champaign, IL: Human Kinetics.

Torbert, M. 1996. *Follow me: A handbook of movement activities for children.* Philadelphia: Leonard Gordon Institute for Human Development Through Play of Temple University.

About the Author

Brian J. Barrett, PhD, has worked as an elementary physical educator since 1979. Currently a teacher, Barrett has presented in numerous workshops at the local, state, national, and international levels. A member of AAHPERD (American Alliance for Health, Physical Education, Recreation and Dance), the American College of Sports medicine, and the North American Society for Pediatric Exercise Medicine, Barrett has contributed numerous articles in a variety of professional journals and conducted research on the physiological and psychological contributions of selected low-organization games. Barrett lives in Freehold, New Jersey, with his wife, Monica, her son Michael, their daughter Rose, and his mother, Lois.